bookworks

bookworks

BOOKS, MEMORY AND PHOTO ALBUMS, JOURNALS, AND DIARIES MADE BY HAND

SUE DOGGETT

WATSON-GUPTILL PUBLICATIONS
NEW YORK

A QUINTET BOOK

First published in the United States in 1998 by
Watson-Guptill Publications, a division of BPI
Communications, Inc., 1515 Broadway,
New York, N.Y. 10036

Library of Congress Cataloging-in-Publication data
Doggett, Sue.
    Bookworks : books, memory and photo albums,
  journals, and diaries made by hand / Sue Doggett.
        p.   cm.
    Includes bibliographical references and index.
    ISBN 0-8230-0491-0 (cloth)
    1. Bookbinding.   2. Bookbinding—United States.   I.
Title.
  Z271.D57 1998
686.3—dc21
                                98-22960
                                CIP

This book was designed and produced by
Quintet Publishing Limited
6 Blundell Street
London N7 9BH

Creative Director: Richard Dewing
Art Director: Clare Reynolds
Designer: Paul Wood
Project Editor: Toria Leitch
Editor: Maggie McCormick
Photographer: Jon Bouchier
Illustrator: Sue Doggett

Manufactured in Singapore
Printed in China

contents

about this book

THE BOOK IS A VERY FAMILIAR, TACTILE, and interactive object that can be a pleasure to hold, read, and write in, especially when it is made well from beautiful and unusual materials.

This book shows you, through step-by-step instructions, **diagrams, and full-color illustrations,** **how you can make your own bookworks using a** myriad of wonderful papers, cloths, and found materials.

There are chapters dealing with simple folded books, pamphlet stitches, more complex multisection bindings, and containers, all of which can be combined to create your own personalized journals, notebooks, albums, and portfolios. There are gallery sections included for inspiration, with examples of work by practicing book artists, binders, and students, which show ways in which the projects described throughout the book can be developed. The first half of this book deals with getting started, making your own decorative papers, basic techniques, and an introduction to different types of book forms, while the remaining sections are given over to specific projects. The projects involve many new structures and techniques while at the same time utilizing and building upon skills acquired in the earlier chapters. You need only a few basic tools and papers to get started, but of course you can expand your tool box and storage area at a later date if you get really hooked! Hopefully this book will act as a starting point, a springboard for ideas and creative development.

If you need extra information on bookbinding books, and where to buy materials, there is a list of suppliers and useful addresses at the back of the book, and a selected bibliography for further reading.

what is a book?

THE HISTORY OF THE BOOK IS RICH and varied, and so closely linked with the development of language, technology, and culture that it could be said to be a mirror of society and its history.

The story of the book goes hand in hand with that of writing. From the earliest times, people have always found ways to leave their mark. In the past, all kinds of materials have been used to write on; clay, papyrus, bones, wooden tablets, tree bark, palm leaves, and animal skins (notably leather, which is a traditional bookbinding material) have all been used to record information. The earliest examples of clay tablets found were from the Great Temple at Uruk in Sumeria. They date from the fourth millennium BC, and are written in cuneiform, a system of writing into wet clay using a wedge-shaped stylus. The Egyptians, famous for their hieroglyphs and papyrus, had been writing since around the thirteenth century BC, and the earliest surviving papyrus is about 5,000 years old. The earliest example of Chinese writing is inscribed on bone and belongs to the fourteenth century BC, but the most important development attributed to the Chinese concerning the history of the book is the invention of paper in AD 105. Paper remained a closely guarded secret, and took many years to reach the West, where parchment (often in the form of highly prized, rare, and exclusive illuminated manuscripts) was the most common writing material for books. Paper reached the West via the Silk Route through Turkestan, Syria, and Persia; and papermaking factories were set up in Samarkand and Baghdad. Papermaking finally reached Spain in the eleventh century, France in the twelfth century, Fabriano in Italy (still famous today for its handmade paper) in 1268 and England in the 1490s. The invention of movable type is attributed to Johannes Gutenburg in the fifteenth century, although the Chinese already had type in the eleventh century. This invention combined with the use of paper, changed the course of book production forever. Books became cheaper, more portable, and therefore available to more people than ever before. During the following centuries and particularly after the invention of the mechanical press and the papermaking machine in the late eighteenth and early nineteenth centuries, there was a print explosion. Printing on a handpress could produce 300 sheets a day in the 1780s, while the four-cylinder press invented in 1828 could produce 4,000 sheets an hour.

Books have gone through many changes in form over the centuries, to become the structures we now commonly recognize. Coming full circle, we have begun to look again at archaic book forms as a source of inspiration and of reinvention, a counter-argument to using the book as purely a reading machine. To recapture the excitement of handling and reading books is possible by presenting them in an unfamiliar format. They have always been valued for their role in communication and education, and as a record of our varied cultures; but alongside this has been the development of the book as an object of beauty in its own right, encompassing the skills of printers, artists, designers, illustrators, typographers, and bookbinders alike. In recent years, the hand-bound book has enjoyed an increasing popularity among artists and makers as a vehicle for visual and artistic expression. There have been new educational courses and workshops established, artists' book fairs, galleries showing more books, books being written about books, and there is academic discussion, all of which highlight a continuing intellectual and practical interest in the role of the book in this age of the Internet and computer technology.

The history of the book is not just about grand gestures, but personal pleasures, too. The excitement you get from writing or drawing for the first time—in a notebook, sketchbook, or diary that you have made yourself—is greater than anything you'll get from a glossy store-bought one. Even the simplest techniques can produce very satisfying results with unusual combinations of color, texture, and materials. Before making anything however, it is a good idea to start with an introduction to how a book works. Familiarity with the terms commonly used in bookbinding, and a knowledge of how books function, will help you to get the most out of this book and the books you make.

book words

THE PROJECTS IN THIS BOOK ARE BASED around two basic structures, one Western and one Eastern: the codex and the accordion fold. The accordion is a simple, beautiful, and extensive form that is amazingly versatile. The codex book is a more complex structure in terms of binding, and just as exciting to experiment with.

The physical parts of a book are interrelated and they work together to form a structure that has remained essentially unchanged for hundreds of years. The diagram at left shows the various parts of a codex form with a cover. It is a simplified drawing that shows you the main elements of the structure, giving the common names, which are used throughout this book. You will find additional information on technical terms used in book binding in the glossary on the opposite page.

A codex book form consists of a number of sections which are sewn together to form the book block. If a section is printed, or is part of a printed book, it is called a signature. Each section is made from a single sheet of paper, which is folded down and cut to the required size. Each time the paper is folded in half, it is given a different name: folio, quarto, and octavo (A). Suitable papers for the projects in this book, and for bookbinding in general, are suggested later in this chapter, under the heading "Paper."

glossary

ACCORDION Length of paper folded like a fan. Also called concertina, zigzag, or leporello fold.

BACK The edge of the book that is bound.

BEESWAX Applying beeswax to sewing thread makes it easier to sew with and stronger. Pull the thread through a lump of beeswax a couple of times.

BOARDS The cover boards of a book.

BOOK BLOCK The total number of sections making up a book.

CASE Cover of a case-bound book.

CASING-IN Process of pasting a book into a case.

CODEX Book structure sewn in sections along one edge, usually on the fold.

DECKLE EDGE Ragged, feathery edge of a handmade sheet of paper.

ENDPAPER Folded sheets of paper attached to first and last sections of a book for protection. Usually pasted down inside cover boards.

FAN FOLD Narrow accordion fold.

FORE EDGE The edges of the pages at the front of the book (opposite the spine).

GRAIN DIRECTION The direction in which the fibers lay in a piece of machine-made paper.

HEAD The top edge of a book.

JOINT The hinge point on a book where the cover board meets the spine.

JOINT ALLOWANCE The space left between the spine edge of the cover boards and the spine board. Necessary for the cover to open.

KETTLESTITCH From the German word "ketteln," meaning to link or make a chain. Sewn at each end of the sections to hold them together.

PASTE DOWN The outside fold of the endpaper that is pasted to the cover board.

SECTION A folded and cut sheet of paper. Used either singly or as a unit of a multisection book.

SEWING SUPPORT Any tape, cord, or other material that supports the sewing of a book. Usually attached or laced in to the cover.

SPINE The part of a cover that protects the backbone of the book.

SQUARE Board or covering paper that extends beyond, and protects the pages in, the book.

STIPPLING Method of gluing in which you hold a large, round-headed brush vertically and move it up and down over the glued area to remove all long, sweeping brush marks.

TAIL The bottom edge of a book. Also called foot.

TURN-IN Covering material that turns in over the edges of the cover boards.

WASTE PAPER Old newspapers or magazines for gluing up on to protect work and work surfaces.

tools and equipment

YOU WILL NEED A FEW BASIC HAND tools to make most of the projects in this book, and many of them are available from art and craft stores. Some tools can also be found in hardware stores, while a few will need to be bought from specialized outlets. Some of the larger items of equipment listed are optional, and where possible, alternatives have been indicated. However, a bookbinder's press is very useful and using one will give your work a more professional finish. It is sometimes possible to find presses in secondhand shops and flea markets, but they are much sought after, and it may be easier to contact a bookbinding supplier. Some of these tools can be adapted from household utensils or made from scratch. Alternatives and instructions on how to make them are given where appropriate.

Rulers and Straight Edges

Various steel rulers are available with both metric and standard measurements. A safety ruler with a recess for your fingers is advisable, especially when cutting boards.

Cutting Tools

Any craft knife will do for cutting paper, but a scalpel with a separate handle and blade is preferable. The blades become blunt very quickly and often need changing, so a scalpel is ideal. A sharp blade gives you a better cut and you don't need to press so hard, which means your hand is less likely to slip and the blade less likely to snap. The most useful size blade is 10a.

An X-Acto knife has a much thicker, stronger blade and is more suitable for cutting boards.

A clip point knife is useful for cutting folds when preparing sections ready for sewing, but a reasonably sharp, blunt-ended kitchen knife would do instead.

A cutting mat keeps your blades from becoming blunt too quickly and protects the work surface. Mats come in various sizes, and some have grid marks to help you cut materials square.

Clockwise from top: **boards, hole punch, dividers, bone folders, scalpel, bodkin, knife, brushes, straight edge, and Chinese scissors.**

Bone Folders

Useful for scoring and folding paper, rubbing down, turning in corners, and making boxes. They come in various shapes and sizes, but the single most useful type has a point at one end and is rounded at the other.

Dividers

Dividers enable you to make accurate measurements. Spring dividers that screw open and closed, staying set in the position you require, are the best type to buy.

Drawing Square

This is for checking before and after cutting that cover boards and other materials are square.

Needles

Bookbinder's size 18 is a good needle to work with, but any long needle with a large eye would be suitable. Curved upholstery needles are useful for winding thread around cords already sewn onto the spine.

Brushes

A large paste brush is essential, and it can be used for gluing and pasting, provided you wash it out well after using craft glue. Smaller brushes for gluing spines and board edges and applying decoration are always useful.

Scissors

You probably already have a large pair of general-purpose scissors around the house, and perhaps a smaller pair such as embroidery scissors or Chinese scissors like the pair pictured are useful, for cutting threads and more delicate work.

Pencils and Erasers

It is better to use an HB pencil, or softer, for marking books and paper. The harder grades (H to 6H), leave impressions which are more difficult to erase. Always keep your pencils sharp for a more accurate measurement.

Bodkin or Awl

Either is useful for making sewing holes in sections and piercing boards for ties and cords. You can make a bodkin by drilling a hole in the end of a small piece of doweling and gluing a needle into the hole.

Hammer and Chisel

For making slits for tapes and ties in cover boards, etc. You can use a craft knife, but do NOT let it slip.

Small Hand Drill

Useful for making holes through thicker boards for sewing on tapes, etc.

Hole Punch and Eyelet Maker

For making and finishing holes for ties, ribbons, and album posts, etc.

Pressing Boards

A few pairs of wooden boards in various sizes, if possible. Make sure the surface of your pressing boards is completely smooth; any lumps or bumps may mark your finished work, especially when it is damp.

Weights

Anything heavy. Books will do, but better still, look out for old flat irons or lead weights. You can also use covered bricks. Remember, the more even the pressure, the better the pressing.

Presses

Bookbinding presses come in various sizes, from small nipping presses to very large standing presses. They are often made of cast iron, but you may also find wooden and aluminum ones.

Paper Cutter

A small paper cutter with a safety bar and a clamp can be useful for trimming book edges, but it is not essential. Most books will look good with roughly cut edges, or with the deckle edge of handmade paper left untrimmed. You can trim your sections to size with a sharp scalpel before sewing if you wish.

materials

Boards

Many of the projects in this book require boards, for covers and for box-making. You can use almost any cardboard or mat board as long as it is thick enough, especially when you are trying out new projects or practicing techniques. However, the best boards to use for finished work are bookbinder's greyboard and millboard. They are both made from good-quality compressed waste and recycled paper. Millboard is denser, tougher, and hot-rolled, which means it has a very smooth surface. The less expensive greyboard is excellent for all the projects in this book. Boards come in various thicknesses, ranging from ³⁄₁₆ inch to about ⅛ inch, the most useful being about ⅛ inch.

Millboard and greyboard are usually acid-free, but for conservation purposes, archival millboard is guaranteed acid-free and buffered with an agent that stops it from picking up acid from the atmosphere.

Cloth

There is a wide choice of bookbinder's cloth that can be bought by the yard from bookbinding suppliers. Cloth used for covering books and boxes is more hard-wearing than paper, but the choice of color is much smaller. Some cloths have a waterproof surface that means they can be cleaned; others resemble canvas or fabric. Other fabrics can be used for covering, but if they are

thin or the weave is loose, you will need to apply a backing fabric or paper. This will stop any adhesive from seeping through and spoiling the look of your work. Backing can be applied to the fabric using fusible webbing, or by gluing a thin piece of paper with craft glue.

Lining Materials

The materials most commonly used to line the spines of books after sewing are mull, linen, and kraft paper. Mull is an open-weave material stiffened with sizing and is used for strengthening spines, usually in case bindings. Linen is stronger than mull and can be used in the same way. It can also be sewn onto the spine of a pamphlet for a more durable binding. Kraft paper is used for lining spines, boards, and boxes, and it is strong and inexpensive. Although the usual color is brown, it does come in other colors and can be used for artwork and for covering books.

Sewing Materials

You can use all sorts of tapes, thread, cords, and ribbons for sewing. Sewing supports depend on your design and what the book is going to be used for. The best thread for strength is bookbinder's linen thread, which is made from flax fiber and comes in various thicknesses. It is usually cream in color, being unbleached, but you can also buy it in black. If your sewing is going to show and you want a splash of color, use button thread and apply some beeswax. For case bindings, the best supports to use are linen or cotton fabric tape, which are sold by the roll. Linen tape is unbleached and made from woven flax fiber, while cotton tape is usually bleached. Where the sewing supports are going to show or be part of the design, you can let your imagination run wild. Anything from the notions counter can be used, including leather thongs, ribbons, and rubber piping, as long as they are reasonably strong. With all materials, bear in mind what you are going to do with the book and how it is going to be used. The stronger the materials, the longer the book will last.

Found Materials

There are any number of found or easily acquired materials that can be used to enhance your book-works and boxes. They are often free or cost very little and can be found around the house, in junk and hardware stores, and when you're out and about. Curiously twisted driftwood can be used alongside raffia and garden twine as fastenings for journals and albums, and a treasure trove of beads for sewing and finishing can be discovered at local thrift shops and secondhand stores. Leaves, wire mesh, carved erasers, and combs can be inked and used to print decorative papers, and scraps of treasured handmade paper can be collaged or sewn together for use as an alternative covering material. Copper and brass wire can be used to decorate clasps, and little pieces of doweling or wooden skewers make wonderful toggles when carved, or painted and polished. Explore the projects in this book and look at the found materials that have been used, particularly in the Scrapbook, the Diary with a Clasp and the gallery pages, which will give you a place to start. Be as inventive as you dare, start collecting, and above all, don't throw anything away. It could end up on a book!

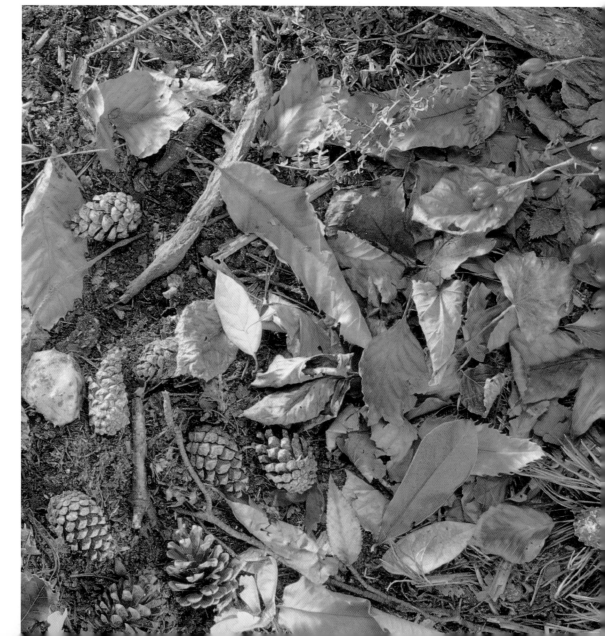

Utility Papers

These are papers used for protection, linings, pressing, and wrapping. It is advisable to keep a stock of these papers, many of which can be used more than once, as they will help keep your work clean and give it a better finish.

1. BLOTTING PAPER

This is used for absorbing the dampness from newly pasted endpapers, linings, and papers that have been laminated with paste. It can be dried out after use and reused.

2. WAXED PAPER

Keep your work clean and free of glue by using any kind of waxy, silicone-release, greaseproof, or plastic-coated paper (such as the backing from self-adhesive covering film) or even sheets of plastic film.

3. TISSUE

Acid-free tissue paper is inexpensive and available from paper and bookbinding suppliers. It is a good way of keeping your work clean when it is finished and as interleaving for albums, etc.

4. NEWSPRINT

Good for gluing and pasting up delicate work and light-colored books that will show the dirt.

5. OLD NEWSPAPERS AND MAGAZINES

Keep plenty of these for general gluing and pasting. Less print comes off the color sections of newspapers and magazines, so they are probably better.

Adhesives

There are two types of adhesive used for the projects in this book: wheatflour paste and craft glue.

1. CRAFT GLUE

Craft glue is widely available at craft shops, art supply stores, and bookbinding suppliers. It is used for general bookbinding work, case making, applying covering materials, and gluing spines. There are lots of different brands available, but the best bookbinding quality is more flexible than some of the others. It is sold in both an ordinary and a reversible version.

2. WHEATFLOUR PASTE

This paste is used in bookbinding and conservation as it penetrates well due to the high water content. It is also colorless and reversible, which means you can remove it with water. Paste is generally used for laminating two papers together and for putting down endpapers. You can make your own paste at home by following this recipe:

INGREDIENTS

2 rounded tablespoons of plain wheat flour

2 cups of cold water

METHOD

1. Add a little of the water to the flour and mix to a smooth paste. Add the water little by little to prevent lumps from forming. Keep adding the water until it is all mixed in. If you prefer, the flour and water can be mixed in a blender.

2. Transfer the mixture to a non-metal saucepan (traces of metal can cause paper to deteriorate over time) and slowly bring to a boil, stirring continuously. The paste will thicken. Reduce the heat and cook for a couple of minutes stirring all the time.

3. Transfer the paste to a container, cover it to stop a skin from forming, and leave it to cool. It will keep in the refrigerator for about a week. If you find the paste is too thick, it can be thinned with water, mixing well.

paper

Paper is usually the main component of a book, so it is worth spending some time looking at what it is and how it is made.

The invention of paper is generally attributed to a Chinese emperor's eunuch called Ts'ai Lun, in AD 105. Previously books had been made from silk fibers, but he began the process of using beaten fibers, originally hemp and bark, which is the main characteristic of paper.

Paper is made from cellulose, which is derived from broken-down plant fibers such as cotton—with 100 percent cellulose, it is one of the best materials for papermaking—hemp, wood, and flax. Paper was made entirely by hand until the 1800s, when the demand for it increased. Refined wood pulp became a cheaper, more plentiful alternative to cotton, and a papermaking machine was invented to speed up the process. The difference between makes and types of paper is vast, and their uses are many and various. Paper can be purchased from art supply stores, craft shops, and specialist suppliers, and you can probably buy basic typing paper from your local convenience store. If you can visit one of the larger paper shops or warehouses, you'll be overwhelmed by the splendor and diversity of the papers available from all over the world.

When you are starting out on the first projects, just about any paper will get you going.

A good-quality typing paper is a basic material for pages and sections. If you want to use acid-free paper, check the content, since not all papers are. A high acid content usually means the paper is not particularly resistant to light or the atmosphere, and over time will deteriorate more quickly than a paper with a neutral pH value. Acid-free is about 7pH, a balance of acid and alkali. Paper can be divided into three main areas: handmade, machine-made, and mold-made paper. The method of production for each type of paper is different, and the resulting paper has very distinct characteristics.

Handmade Paper

The process of hand forming sheets of paper has remained the same for hundreds of years. The fibers are beaten and suspended in water, then removed using a mold and frame called a deckle.

The papermaker moves the mold back and forth to disperse the fibers and then lets the water drain off. After this, the sheet of paper is transferred to a piece of felt or blanket which is called "couching." When enough sheets are piled up between felts, they are pressed to remove the remainder of the water and left to dry. The choice of papers available from the mills of Europe, Japan, and India are extraordinary in their variety and beauty. There are special papers for printmaking and drawing, and all kinds of colors, textures, and designs are available to the book artist. Some papers, such as the Indian Khadi type, include materials as diverse as wool, banana leaf, algae, and various grasses, each having an individual appearance. There are Japanese papers with gold flecks and long, silky, swirling fibers, such as Unryu. There are also varieties of paper which are not really paper at all, such as papyrus, made by overlaying crosswise strips of the stem of the papyrus plant, and Amate which is made from beaten bark (from Mexico and central America), that are ancient in origin. The creative possibilities of all of these papers is endless. Handmade paper is exciting and rewarding to work with, and although there is a considerable difference in cost between the cheapest and most expensive paper, you can build up a stock of beautiful materials without spending a lot.

Machine-made Paper

The process of producing paper on a machine is very different from that of handmade paper, and its uses are mainly commercial. The most common source of fiber used in machine papermaking is chemically treated wood pulp. The pulp is placed on a moving bed and is then pressed through a series of rollers and felts. From here the paper is put through a drying machine. It is then sized and dried again before being wound onto a roll, after which it is cut into individual sheets. The sizing (which is also added to handmade paper) can be made from gelatin, starch, or other chemical compounds. It makes the paper water-resistant and suitable for writing and printing on. There are plenty of machine-made papers useful for making books, and many manufacturers make highly colored, light-resistant, and acid-free lines. Mold-made papers are made on a cylinder machine, but the preparation of the high-grade pulp is the same as for handmade paper.

Grain Direction

There is one characteristic of machine-made paper that is technically very important to the construction of the book. Paper is made on a continuously moving bed, not in individual sheets so the fibers tend to flow in one direction. This is called the grain direction. If the paper becomes damp—through pasting or gluing, for example—the fibers stretch in the cross direction, at right angles to the grain direction. As the paper dries, it shrinks back and creates a "pull" on anything the paper is stuck to. It is necessary to control the effects of this pull when binding books so that they are strong and function well. All the materials in a book should have the grain direction running from head to tail, especially on the boards and endpapers where control of the stretch is most vital. Paper folds better with the grain, the pages will open more easily. There are various ways to test for the grain direction:

1. Fold the paper in half lengthwise, without creasing it, and apply gentle pressure. Then, fold the paper widthwise and feel the difference in the resistance. One way will be springier than the other. The fold with the least resistance is the direction of the grain.

2. Tear a small strip from the corner of a sheet of paper and wet it. The paper will curl because the fibers are expanding. The grain runs in the opposite direction from the curl of the paper.

3. Hold the corner of a piece of paper and pull one edge through the nails of your thumb and index finger in order to stretch it. Do the same with the other edge. The grain direction runs parallel to the edge which stretches the least.

decorating paper

When decorating paper, there are a few qualities that will determine how your finished piece will look. For example, textured and smooth papers will have contrasting finishes, and an absorbent paper will behave totally differently from a coated one. To test the absorbency of a paper, wet the corner of your sheet and see how long it takes for the water to disappear. The quicker it goes, the more absorbent the paper. When selecting papers, choose those with qualities that you find appealing, such as their texture, color, fragility, or strength, and experiment with the following techniques to make your own personalized covering materials. All the techniques described below can be used alone or with one another to create a host of unusual decorative effects.

MATERIALS

A selection of papers

Watercolors, poster paint, acrylics, and drawing inks

Water-based block-printing ink for monoprinting

Found objects and materials for printing with

Paste for paste papers

Masking fluid

TOOLS

Print rollers for applying color

Brushes and toothbrushes for painting and spattering

Jars for mixing and storing paint

Wooden skewers and paint brush ends for drawing into paste papers (explained below)

Cardboard scraps with comb-cut edges for decorating paste papers

Thick sheet of plastic or a piece of glass for inking up

An eye dropper for sprinkling color (optional)

TECHNIQUES

Sprinkling

1. DRY METHOD

Using an eye dropper or a paint brush, drip pools of watercolor or ink onto a dry paper, then roll the paper in various directions to run the color.

2. WET METHOD

Run cold water over your sheet of paper and then drip color onto the wet areas. It will spread and bleed, giving a spidery effect.

Spattering

Alternatively, using the same techniques as above, use a toothbrush and a knife to sprinkle paint onto the paper for a more delicate effect.

Crumpling and Wash-off

If you crumple the paper carefully after coloring, the ink will settle in the creases, giving an "antique" feel. Be careful not to use too many different colors at once or you could end up with everything sludge-colored.

If you let the paint dry a little and then rinse the paper under the faucet, you can obtain other interesting effects. The wash-off method can be used with most of the techniques described here. You will find that some paints stain the paper—which is yet another effect to experiment with.

Masking Out

Paint or spatter masking fluid onto your paper (use smooth paper as the fluid will come off more easily) and let it dry. Paint watercolor washes (watered-down color) over the top, and when they are dry, rub off the masking fluid with an eraser. You will be left with the original paper showing through, which you can either leave or cover with another wash.

Paste Papers

Paste papers are a traditional way of decorating book covers and are fun to make. You will need jars for various colors of poster paint, pieces of cardboard with teeth cut along one edge, and blunt tools to draw with. Make a quantity of paste as described in the Adhesives section. Mix one quarter paint to three quarters paste. Use a less absorbent paper for this technique.

Using broad brush strokes, paint the paste mixture onto the paper thinly and evenly. Using any of the drawing tools or cardboard combs, draw into the paste. The color of the base paper will show through where you have drawn. If you don't like what you've done, simply brush over the paste and start again.

Dyeing

The paper for this method should be thin and absorbent, like a strong tissue or Japanese paper. Fold the paper into a zigzag, and then fold this zigzag into another so you end up with a square. Have a few paint colors mixed in jars and dip each corner or edge of the folded paper into the jars alternately. Open up the folded paper, lay it flat, and leave it to dry.

Printing

You can use any of the following methods to print paper you have already colored using other techniques.

1. MONOPRINTING

Use an ink roller to cover a smooth surface like a piece of plastic or glass with block printing ink. Then draw into it with the end of a paint brush. Lay a piece of paper on top of the paint and rub over it with the back of a spoon or your hand. When you peel the paper off, you will have a reverse image of your drawing, called a monoprint because you can only take one print. Making a second printing will sometimes work, but it will be much fainter.

2. PRINTING WITH A ROLLER AND FOUND OBJECTS

Tie string around your roller and then ink up on a piece of glass or plastic. When the roller is inked all around, roll it over your paper and the string print will be transferred. Alternatively, ink up bottle rims, screen wire, leaves, etc., and print by

pressing them down onto your paper.

3. RUBBER STAMPS

Using large plastic erasers to make stamps can produce exciting repeated designs and patterns that look good as borders or for covers and endpapers. Draw your image, a simple shape or letter, on the eraser and cut out the negative areas with a craft knife. Cut away at an angle from the edge of your design so the base is wider than the area you are going to print which will stop the eraser collapsing. Using a stamp pad (available in various colors), print the design on your paper.

Collage

1. PASTING PAPERS

Scraps of paper can be pasted on a full sheet to produce an image or an abstract design. If you are going to use the collage to cover a book or for folding, thinner papers are better because this technique gives two thicknesses of paper laminated together. You can use craft glue or paste to attach the scraps. Paste is probably better, even though it takes longer to dry, because it leaves no residue and can be cleaned off easily. Try photocopying images and designs, and then enlarging or reducing parts of them. Play around with your own drawings and prints by tearing and repositioning them.

2. SEWING PAPERS

Papers can be sewn together either by hand or with machine embroidery. Thinner papers are better if you want to fold the paper at all, but otherwise it is up to you. There are plenty of exciting sewing threads to experiment with,

especially metallic or brightly dyed ones, and some embroidery threads are dyed with different colors on the same skein. You can make it as simple or exotic as you like by varying color schemes. Try using different papers of the same color with contrasting stitching, or multicolored strips or circles or abstract forms. The permutations are endless.

Do's and Don'ts

There are no rules really, but a few hints will help you make sure you get the most out of your tools and materials, and that your work stays looking good when you've finished it.

THINGS TO REMEMBER:

1. If you use acrylic paint to make a print or design, make sure you always have the work wrapped in waxed paper, especially when it is stuck to the book. Acrylic will stick to itself or anything else when it is damp or under pressure.

2. If you are making a paper for a particular project, keep in mind where the paper is going to be used. If it needs to be pliable, then use a medium or lighter-weight paper and so on.

3. If you can afford it, buy separate brushes for different jobs to reduce the risk of getting old paint or glue where you don't want it. Always make sure you wash your brushes thoroughly after using any paint and especially after using craft glue.

folded books

FOLDED BOOKS, SOMETIMES CALLED ACCORDIONS, CONCERTINAS, OR leporellos, originally developed from the scroll form. Scrolls were awkward to read because they had to be continually unwound and rewound in order to locate specific passages. By folding the length of cloth, paper, or papyrus into a zigzag and forming pages, reading became a much simpler task. The folded book has been widely used in Japan and the Far East for many centuries, with some of the most beautiful and delicate examples being the "flutter" books made from rice or other fine papers. Paper was not the only material used for making folded books. In India and Sumatra birch bark was very popular up until the end of the 1800s, and even old stiffened clothes were folded up and used for making account books.

From simple accordion pleating to the **more complex star structures described** later in this book, these forms are functional and fun.

They can be used in many ways: as notebooks, journals, and albums; to make exciting greeting cards by adding illustrations and text; or as beautiful free-standing sculptural forms.

In this section you will learn the easy way to fold a perfect accordion, how to make books with and without glue, and how to develop your own style by experimenting with unusual folds.

how to fold an accordion

THE EASIEST WAY TO FOLD THE PERFECT ZIGZAG IS ALWAYS TO BEGIN FOLDING INTO THE CENTER, not from one end which may seem more obvious. First, decide how wide you want each fold to be and multiply this measurement by how many folds you want. Sticking to an even number of folds makes it easier to measure. A fold is a division of a length of paper with a crease down the center. For example, if each fold is 4 inches wide and you want four folds, then the total length of your paper should be 16 inches.

Fold the paper in half widthwise (A). Then take one end (B) and fold it into the middle (A).

Fold the crease line at (C) back on itself and then match it up with the original fold line (A).

Then take the end (B) and fold up to crease (C). Repeat with the other half of the accordion.

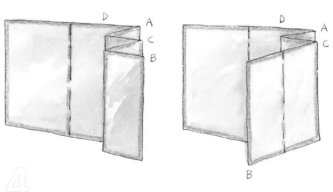

If your paper is not long enough to fold an accordion to the required size, you can extend it. To join two lengths, take two pieces of paper the size you need. On one, allow an extra ¼ to ⅜ inch at one end. Crease along this point and fold over. Now fold both accordions as described above. When this is done, glue or paste the small hinge of paper and attach it to the back of the second fold (C).

pocket fold book

MATERIALS

Paper for covering

Greyboard

Strong paper for the accordion fold

Ribbon, tape, or cord for the ties

Craft glue

Wheatflour paste

Waxed and clean waste paper for pressing

EQUIPMENT

Knife and/or scalpel

Bone folder

Steel safety ruler

Dividers

Chisel, knife, or awl

Hammer

Pressing boards and a weight

Glue brush

ADDING A FOLDED POCKET TO THIS ZIGZAG BOOK will give you extra space for collecting and storing small items. It works like a scrapbook, but because nothing is permanently glued, you can move the contents around or change them completely to suit your needs. You will need to use a fairly strong paper for the pockets to be useful, as they need to stand upright without sagging. The book is closed securely with ties.

1 Decide how tall you want the accordion fold to be (A) and add the required pocket depth (B), making sure the grain direction runs head to tail. Fold up lengthwise to form the pocket (C).

2 Fold up the accordion as described on page 24, keeping the pocket on the outside of the fold.

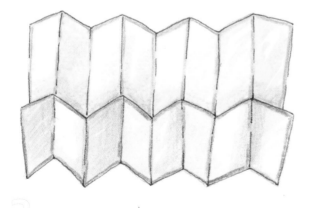

3 For the cover, cut two boards ⅛ inch larger than the accordion fold on all four sides.

4 Cut two pieces of cover paper approximately ¾ inch larger than the cover boards. Put waste paper under the boards and glue (stipple the glue to get a thin, even coat. See Glossary on page 11). Place the board down on the wrong side of the cover paper, turn it over, and rub well with a bone folder or your hand through a piece of clean paper. If you have a press, nip the covered boards between pressing boards and waxed paper for a minute.

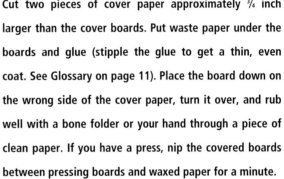

5 Use the dividers, or a ruler and a sharp pencil, to mark the turn-in allowance (A) ⅝ inch out from the edge of the boards. Trim along these points with a craft knife and safety ruler (B).

To cut the corners, first fold each paper corner over the board to form a right angle (A). Lift the corners up again; you now have a 45-degree crease line (B). Allow for the thickness of the board when cutting the corners. If you cut too close, the turn-ins will not meet when you turn them over. Therefore, measure the board thickness with the dividers (adding a bit extra) and transfer this measurement to the outside of the crease line, away from the board edge (C). Now cut along this line (D).

To attach the ties you will need to make a slot in the front board using a hammer and chisel or a strong knife. To do this, you first have to find the halfway point of the board height and mark this point 1 inch in from the board edge (A). Measure the width of your ribbon and transfer this measurement to the board taking point (A) as the center of the line (B). Cut or chisel through the boards onto a pile of waste greyboards to avoid damaging the work surface.

Glue one edge of the turn-in, making sure there is enough adhesive along the board edge. Then turn it over. Rub the paper down along the board edges first to stop any air bubbles forming. Then rub the turn-ins down well (A).

Notice that at either end of the turn-in, there is a small amount of cover paper overlapping the corner of the board (B). This needs to be flattened into the board edge with a bone folder or your thumb to avoid small "ears" of paper forming and to obtain a neat finish. Do this at both ends, then repeat on the opposite side.

Finally glue down the remaining two turn-ins (A) and leave boards to dry between clean paper and pressing boards under a weight.

To measure the ribbon length, first place the accordion fold between the two boards. Cut two lengths of ribbon, one four times the width and one twice the width of the board.

11

Remove the back board and the accordion and push the ribbon through the slit, keeping the longer piece on the left and the shorter one on the right. Glue down about ⅜ inch of each end of the ribbon to the back of the board, on either side of the slit. Hammer flat.

12

Place a piece of waste paper under the front fold of the accordion as protection and paste or glue the surface. Place this pasted side down on the inside of the front cover board, making sure it is central and the pocket fold is at the bottom (A). Repeat for the other side.

13

Open out the folded bottom pocket and pull the ribbons to the front to avoid making any indentations while the book is being pressed. Place waxed paper over the pasted boards and leave them to dry under a weight between paper and pressing boards.

14

When the book is dry (leave overnight if possible), re-fold the bottom pocket and run a little glue along the edge at each end (A). Glue to secure the pocket fold.

15

To finish, take the longer ribbon around the back of the closed book and tie at the fore edge.

everlasting fold book

THE BEAUTY OF THIS BOOK IS ITS SIMPLICITY. There is very little to glue, and the cover papers are wrapped around the boards. The accordion fold is slotted into the cover, so when one fold is full of notes, sketches, or shopping lists, it can be removed and replaced with another. This book could be used as a diary or notebook, with the wraparound cover making a handy place for keeping scraps and ephemera, such as wine labels and tickets, until they find a more permanent home. The fold can be as long as you like, but you may need to join sheets of paper together using the method described earlier.

MATERIALS

Cover paper—plain or decorative, medium-weight

Greyboard

Paper for the accordion fold

Craft glue

EQUIPMENT

Knife and/or scalpel

Steel safety ruler

Dividers

Drawing square

Cutting mat or board

Small glue brush

1 Fold an accordion to the required size, not too big to start with.

2 Using a knife and the safety ruler, cut two boards slightly larger than the folded accordion (A). Use a drawing square or the cutting mat grid to make sure the boards have right angles at each corner, and make sure the grain direction runs from top to bottom (B).

3 Cut two pieces of cover paper the same height as the boards (A) and twice the width (B), adding ⅜ inch for an overlap (C).

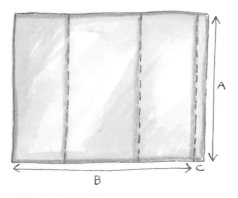

4 Wrap the paper around the boards, add a little glue along the edge of the narrower turn-in and overlap this with the wider one (A).

Cut a piece of cover paper for the spine; the same height as the boards (A), and the same width as the accordion fold (B). Measure the width of the spine by creasing it around the folded pages (C) or by using dividers. Leave ¾ inch of paper to each side of the creases; this will be attached to the boards.

Run a little glue along the edge of the spine piece (A), line up one of the creased edges with the edge of the board, and glue in place.

Place the accordion in position, run a little glue along the other edge of the spine piece, fold it around the book, and place the second board exactly over the top of the first. Open the boards, take out the accordion, and rub glued areas down well.

Cut two pieces of cover paper, twice the length of the board (A) and the same width (B).

Wrap this cover paper lengthwise around the boards, and tuck the overlap in at the head and tail (A & B). If you find it difficult to tuck in the overlap, cut it a little shorter.

To complete the book, slot the last folds at each end of the accordion (A) into each edge of the inside cover (B).

experimenting with folds

THE FOLLOWING DIAGRAMS AND ILLUSTRATIONS SHOW VARIATIONS ON THE BASIC ACCORDION FOLD.

Using papers of different weights, try folding them, and see how they behave. The thin, more fragile folds of the flutter book have a different quality to the slotted zigzag made of thin cardboard. What happens if you fold the paper at an angle, or slit one of the creases and fold in another direction? Different types of folding can be used to illustrate a poem or short story, or to create a complex maze.

The best way to become familiar with your materials is by handling them, so try a few experimental folds of your own by doodling with some inexpensive paper.

FLUTTER BOOK

Using a very thin paper such as onion skin Japanese, or bank paper, fold an extra-long zigzag. Join the folds as required and attach to a three-part board structure (described in the foldout book on pages 31-33). See also illustrated reference in the Gallery on pages 34-35.

SLOTTED ZIGZAG BOOK

Take two pieces of stiff paper or thin cardboard cut to the same size. Score with a bone folder along the broken lines (see diagram) and make cuts half the height of the paper in the center of each fold. Fold as a zigzag, turn one upside-down and slot together.

ALTERNATIVE FOLDS

Fold a flat piece of paper in half lengthwise, then fold widthwise into quarters. Open out the paper and make a slit down the middle, leaving the top fold intact (A). Fold the paper as a zigzag, starting at number one and ending at number eight.

If you fold the zigzags unevenly, you can sculpt any number of structures. You may need to shape the lower edge (B) if you want it to stand up.

This fold is more complex (C) and the creases need to be measured and scored with a bone folder. Each crease line is folded both ways and then a little patience is needed to coax the folds into position. The solid and broken lines indicated show folds and reverse folds respectively.

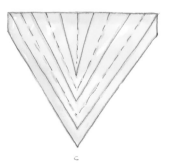

foldout book

THIS BOOK IS INSPIRED BY A VELLUM FIFTEENTH-CENTURY DOCTOR'S NOTEBOOK and diagnostic chart in the British Library. Fold-outs are useful for maps, plans, and charts and they could be an unusual way of displaying artwork. Instead of storing prints and drawings in a portfolio, why not fold them into pocket-sized bookworks?

MATERIALS

Paper or artwork for making the fold

Cover paper or bookcloth

Board lining paper (to complement cover paper and fold)

Greyboard

Scrap paper for making a pattern

Wheatflour paste

Craft glue

EQUIPMENT

Bone folder

Knife and/or scalpel

Steel safety ruler

Dividers

Cutting mat or board

Glue brush

Drawing square

Pressing boards and a weight

1

To work out the design of your folds, experiment with scrap paper first. When you have finalized your design, transfer the fold lines to the project paper and score with a bone folder. The more folds you want, the thinner the paper should be. Try to avoid folding the paper too many times as it may crease badly, especially at the corners.

2

In this example, the bottom left-hand section of the paper (A) will be pasted to the cover board. The vertical folds are made first (B) and then the zigzag is folded in half (C).

Measure and cut two boards ⅛ inch bigger than the folded book on all four sides. Place the book inside the boards and use scrap paper folded around the boards to measure for the covering material. Cut the paper or cloth ¾ inch larger than the boards all the way around (A) and crease along the board edges at the spine (B).

If the paper fold is ⅜ inch thick or more, it is a good idea to add a spine lining to the cover for additional strength. The spine lining is often made from kraft paper, but most medium-weight papers will do. If the folded paper is really thick, you can use the same material as the cover boards. Cut a strip of lining paper the same height as the board and the same width as the paper fold down the spine. Put to one side.

Glue one board to the covering material with craft glue and rub it down well. Place the book fold centrally on the glued board.

Glue the second board and place it, glued side up, over the top of the first board. Holding the board with the tips of your fingers, bring the cloth over the top, making sure it fits tightly at the spine.

Before rubbing down, drop the board back and use a ruler to check that the boards are level. Work quickly before the glue dries, in case you need to move the board slightly to straighten it. Glue the spine lining paper and place it centrally between the two boards. Rub down well.

8

Fold, measure, and cut the corners of the covering material (see page 26). Glue the turn-ins over the board edges and across the spine lining, rubbing down well between the boards into the joints (A). Remember to flatten the overlapping paper at the corners before turning in the adjacent edges. Leave to dry between clean paper and pressing boards under a weight.

9

Cut a piece of your chosen lining paper, 1/8 inch smaller than the cover on all four sides.

10

Paste the paper, and starting at one end, glue it to the inside of the boards. Make sure that the paper fits snugly into the central joint or the cover will not open properly. Leave to dry flat as described previously.

11

Paste the bottom folded section ((A) in step 2) of the book and attach centrally to the back cover board. Place a piece of waxed paper over this fold and close the book. Leave to dry overnight (or until the paste is completely dry) between pressing boards under a weight.

From left to right:

Mary Deakin's "Tyger, Tyger" is an accordion book, screen-printed and then over-printed to give an impression of the tiger's speed. The folds are slotted through with torn paper strips.

Sue Doggett's "Electric Eel Book" is made from two accordion folds. The artwork is supported by a windowed accordion, attached by tabs.

Sue Doggett's "The Cheese Museum" is an accordion book printed with text that snakes and meanders around each of the folds. The folds have been creased unevenly to suggest people standing in a queue.

Sue Doggett's "Flutter Book" is made from Japanese paper with paper covered boards. Instructions for making this type of book are described fully on page 30.

Sue Doggett's "Foldout Book" has pages made from one folded sheet of paper, much like a map. Full instructions on how to make it are given on pages 31-33.

pamphlet sewing

PAMPHLET STITCH, ONE OF THE SIMPLEST METHODS OF SEWING, is based around three holes. The thread can be hidden, illustrated in the wraparound book on the following pages, or visible as part of the design.

Pamphlet bindings can be fastened together **with colored sewing thread,** cord, ribbon, raffia, and even shoelaces.

If you want to make a larger book, increase the number of sewing holes to five, seven, or more, or add an extra section to give you more pages and introduce a folded cover with a pleat. If you want to keep the structure really simple, the cover need only consist of two or three folds of paper with the sewing reduced to one central hole, a perfect way to make elegant personalized greeting cards.

To make a basic card or booklet, take one or two folds of your chosen paper and make a hole halfway. Then take a piece of matching or contrasting cord or ribbon and thread it through the hole from the outside. Take the ribbon over the top of the folds and finish off by going back through the central hole and around the bottom so that both ends of the ribbon are on the outside. Tie a bow to secure it and trim the ends at an angle to stop them from fraying.

wraparound book

THIS SIMPLY SEWN BOOK HAS AN EXTENDED COVER which adds strength without weight. Try using a decorative paper with contrasting endleaves, or perhaps handmade paper and colored pages. The cover can contain a hidden message or secret artwork which can be seen only when it is fully open.

MATERIALS
Cover paper
Paper for endleaves
Paper for pages
Sewing thread

EQUIPMENT
Knife and/or scalpel
Steel safety ruler
Needle
Dividers
Bodkin awl or handled needle
Cutting mat

1

Divide the page paper in half to make folds. You will need about six folds of a medium-weight typing paper, or slightly thinner paper if you want extra pages.

2

Cut two folds of colored or decorative paper for endleaves the same size as the page folds. Wrap these around the book.

3

If you want to make the fore edge neater, trim it now with a scalpel and safety ruler.

4

Cut a piece of cover paper the same height, and five times the width of a page. Fold one end around the back of the book (A).

A

5

To prepare for sewing, take a piece of waste paper the same height as the book and divide it into four. The easiest way to do this is to fold the paper in half widthwise as on the previous page, open it up, and then fold each end into the middle and line up with the center crease.

6

Fold the paper in half lengthwise and place it in the center fold of the book. Mark the sewing points where the fold lines intersect. This will be your sewing pattern or guide to follow.

7

From inside, push the needle through the center fold of the book at the three points, making sure the needle comes out exactly on the fold of the cover paper. Remove the paper sewing pattern from the center of the book.

8

Sew the book as follows: From the inside, take the thread through the center hole so it is now on the outside (A). Next, sew through one of the other holes going back into the center (B). Bring the needle out again at the last hole (C). To finish, go back through the center hole, tighten the sewing, and making sure there is a thread on each side of the long stitch, tie a double knot. Cut off the excess thread to about ⅜ inch and close the book. Here the knot appears in the middle of the book. If you don't want the knot to show, begin sewing from the outside.

9

Fold the cover paper back on itself, creasing at the fore edge of the book (A). Then take the paper around the spine and back toward the fore edge, crease again.

A

11

Lay the tab over the inside cover and make a pencil mark on each side of its width.

12

Unfold the cover completely, put a spare piece of board or a cutting mat under the book and cut a slit between the two pencil marks.

10

Cut a tab from the remaining fifth of the cover paper as shown in the diagram. The distance (A) is half the width of a page. (B) is approximately a third of the book's height, but you can make it bigger or smaller as desired.

B

A

13

Refold the cover around the book and insert the tab into the slit. Trim the head and tail of the book with a scalpel to even up the edges if required.

double pamphlet fold with ties

THIS NOTEBOOK IS ALSO SEWN THROUGH THREE HOLES, but an extra section has been added to make more pages. The cover is made from two sheets of paper with a zigzag fold in the center, through which the two sections are attached. The ties are glued between the zigzag fold before sewing and can wrap around the book as many times as you like. You can also make this book without ties, using a colored thread which contrasts with the cover papers, or one which blends to become invisible. Either way, the spine will appear simple and elegant.

MATERIALS

Paper for sections

Paper for inner cover

Medium- to heavyweight cover paper

Sewing thread

Ribbon, tape, etc., for ties

Craft glue

EQUIPMENT

Knife and /or scalpel

Steel safety ruler

Bone folder

Needle

Cutting mat

Small glue brush

1

Fold two sections as in the previous project.

2

Cut another fold of paper for the inner cover. This needs to be the same height as the sections made above and the same width as an opened-out page fold. Add 1½ inches for the zigzag (A). Do the same with the cover paper.

3

Fold both sheets in half and place one inside the other. Measure ¾ inch in from the folded edge. Place a ruler along the measured line (A) and score with a bone folder.

4

Make a sewing pattern on a piece of waste paper as described in the previous project, Wraparound Book.

5

If you want to add ties to your book, cut each one to the required length (at least one and a half times the book width) and attach them inside the zigzag of the cover folds with a little craft glue. The ties should not interfere with the sewing so use your sewing pattern as a guide to avoid these points.

6

Take both folded sections, place them either side of the cover folds, and mark for sewing (A). The sewing holes should go through the folds of both sections and cover papers (B) at the same time.

7

Sew as in the previous project, and finish off with a double knot. Close the book by bringing the covers around to meet the fore edges of the two sections.

five-, seven-, and nine-hole sewing

IF YOU WANT TO MAKE A LARGER book, you may need extra sewing points for strength. Five- and seven-hole sewing is no more complicated than the three-hole method.

METHOD

It works like a figure eight (see below, left). The thing to remember is that you must have one long stitch across the central hole around which you tie the loose threads, and an odd number of holes. Apart from these rules, you can sew with as many holes as you like.

If you place the knot on the outside of the book, it can become the starting point for a design, the simplest example being one-hole ribbon sewing. If you tie a knot instead of a bow and extend the ribbons, you can use them to make ties or tassels, or you can cut slits in the cover paper and thread the ribbon through. The sewing thread or cord can be sewn, knotted, or tied to other materials such as twisted silk, beads, and tassels, all of which can turn this simple but versatile book form into something special. See Gallery Section for some examples of this decorative sewing.

From left to right:

Clare Bryan's "Forbidden Fruit" is a pamphlet stitch book with text and images printed on a variety of papers and tissues, protected within thin wooden boards and a bookcloth spine.

Emma Ruffle and Sue Doggett's "Pamphlets" use simple three hole pamphlet stitching and bark papers, Japanese tissue, and watercolor papers.

Sue Doggett's "Serpents and Skulls" are two small pamphlet stitch books containing printed text and images. They are housed in a simple case, which is made like a photograph frame, and kept in place by two strips of ribbon.

Emma Ruffle's pamphlet bindings are sewn with frayed string and natural materials as design elements.

Sue Doggett's "Pamphlets" have three-, five-, and seven-hole stitching with additional beads and extended threads forming tassels. These formats are described earlier in the chapter, on page 43.

multisection sewing

IF YOU WANT TO MAKE A LARGER BOOK, you will need to add more sections to make a multisection book, or codex. The word codex comes from the Latin *caudex,* meaning "trunk of a tree," and refers to the method used by the Romans to hinge their wooden, wax-filled writing tablets together. From its beginnings as an early type of ring binder, the codex developed into the familiar form we call a book today.

To function as a book, the sections need to be sewn together. Adding sewing supports such as tapes or cords not only makes the structure stronger but also adds visual interest.

This section is divided into two parts. First, all the sewing techniques are described; then, illustrated examples show methods of attaching boards and covers, giving you the opportunity to mix sewing and binding styles to create the book you want.

Sewing is one of the most important structural elements of a book, and it needs to be strong and secure if the book is to be used regularly.

Remember to keep the tension even by constantly tightening up the threads. The best way to do this is to tighten each row of sewing as you go along. If the sewing is loose or uneven, the sections may twist around when the book is being used. This puts a strain on the sewing and could cause the paper to tear.

sewing on tapes

TAPES ARE ADDED TO STRENGTHEN the spine and add decoration. Before sewing, prepare your sections. A good size to start with is probably 6 x 8 inches, which would make a useful notebook. Fold the paper into about eight sections, allowing three to four folds for each. For more pages in your book, add more pages per section and use a thinner paper. Press them between boards under a weight for a few hours, or overnight if you have time. You can leave the torn edges as they are, or you can trim all the sections to the same size before sewing.

MATERIALS

Paper for sections

Linen sewing thread and/or colored threads and silks

Cotton tape, ribbon, cords, thongs, etc., for sewing supports

Beeswax

Scrap paper

EQUIPMENT

Sewing needles

Pencil

Pressing board

Masking tape

Bodkin or handled needle

1 Make the sections square at one end and across the spine. Place them on top of a pressing board.

2 Decide how many tapes you require. For instance, a small book like this could have three or four tapes, while a larger book would probably have more. It also depends on the width of the tape or ribbon, so you might use more thin tapes or fewer thick ones.

3 Tapes should be long enough to cover the spine of the book with overhang of about 2½ to 3 inches. They need to be longer if they are being used for decorative lacing or tying.

4 Make a pencil mark ⅜ to ⅝ inch in from either end of the book where the kettlestitches will be. Divide the space between the kettlestitch points according to the number of tapes being used. Mark with a pencil. The examples below show measuring up for 3 tapes or 4 tapes.

2 TAPES

4 TAPES

5 Place the tapes centrally over the pencil marks and secure with masking tape on the edge of the pressing board.

6

Make a sewing pattern using a folded piece of paper the same length as the sections. Line up the folded edge with the book and mark a point at each end where the kettlestitches are; mark two points, one on either side of each tape.

7

Place the pattern in the center of each section and carefully pierce the sewing holes. Make sure the needle comes out exactly on the fold and not on either side of it.

8

Place the first section on the pressing board, lining up the sewing holes with the tapes. Begin at (A). Take the needle into the center of the first section, then out again at (B), next to the tape. Sew across the tape and go back in through the next hole (C). Continue up to the end hole.

9

Place the second section on top of the first, taking the needle through the end hole. Continue sewing as before. Repeat for the third section.

10

To form the kettlestitch, take the needle to the section below and behind the linking stitch (A). Pull the thread to form a loop, take the needle through the loop, pointing up, and pull tight. Make a kettlestitch at each end of each section, always going down to the section below the one you have just sewn.

11

Complete all the sections. To finish off, make a double kettlestitch into the same hole and snip off the excess thread. Remove the masking tape, turn the book over, and make a double kettlestitch as above on the other side.

12

Remove the pressing board. Close the sewing holes with a needle point to neaten the spine. Add endpapers and attach boards or make a case binding following the directions on pages 58–60 or 62–65.

sewing over cords or thongs

BOOKS WERE TRADITIONALLY SEWN ONTO CORDS OR THONGS, which were covered with leather and appeared as raised bands along the spine. Cord sewing follows the same principles as tape sewing, except you only make one hole per cord. When you sew, the needle goes back into the same hole it came out so the cord is looped. Select your materials from the list on page 48.

Place the sections on a pressing board. Mark the sections and sewing pattern as in figure (A), and put cords in position. Secure them with masking tape (B). The method of sewing and adding sections is the same as for tapes, except at sewing points (C), where the cord is looped. Because of this looping it is necessary to tighten the thread at each cord rather than at the end of each section.

To wrap the cord with extra thread, come out of the sewing hole and wind it around the cord as many times as you need (probably two or three times depending on the thickness of the thread) before going back into the section through the same hole. Be careful not to wind around the cord too many times or the sections will not lay flat.

Finish off as before, with a double kettlestitch.

joining a new thread

IF YOU ARE SEWING MORE THAN three or four sections, you will probably need to join on a new thread at some point. The best way to do this is to make a "weaver's knot," which is very secure and can be positioned exactly. You can join the thread on the inside or the outside of the book, but if your sewing is going to show, then the knot is best hidden inside. Try to avoid joining at the kettlestitch, as this may weaken the sewing.

Make two loops in the new thread.

Take the right-hand loop through the left-hand loop.

Tighten the left-hand loop, but not completely.

Take the old thread through the large loop of the new thread (C) until it is tight around the old thread (B), pull the two ends of the new thread tightly (A). The old thread should "snap" through the loop. Trim the loose ends to about ⅜ inch.

longstitch bindings

IN A LONGSTITCH BINDING, THE SECTIONS AND COVER ARE SEWN SIMULTANEOUSLY, so the sewing becomes part of the design. The longstitches on the spine can be treated in a number of ways, but traditionally they have been wrapped and plaited. You can add beading, silk or metallic threads, and knotting to the stitches as you are sewing, or you can work on them afterward by pinching them together and using embroidery stitches. You can also vary the length and number of stitches you use. Select your materials from the list on page 48.

If you are using paper for the cover, it is a good idea to strengthen the spine fold by gluing on a strip of linen before making the sewing holes. This will stop the paper from tearing and extend the life of the book.

1 Cut, fold, and press sections ready for sewing. Trim to the required size.

2 Cut a piece of scrap paper big enough to wrap loosely around the sections. Add an extra 1¼ inches all around (A). Crease along each side of the backbone of the book to form the spine allowance.

3 Use this pattern to cut your cover paper. Transfer the spine allowance to the cover paper and crease. Allow ⅛ inch extra to form the "square," and 1¼ inches for the "turn-ins" (see glossary on page 11 for an explanation of these terms). Score and crease.

4 Mark and pierce the sewing holes in the cover paper. Divide the distance between (A) and (B) into seven equal parts. This will give you six equally spaced sewing points. Pierce the paper at these points and then pierce holes horizontally across the spine, making a sewing hole for each section. Continue for each of the six sewing points.

5

For clarity the turn-in allowance does not show on the diagrams. Begin sewing from inside the first section, coming out through the cover at the second hole from the end (A). Sew running stitches in and out of the cover and the section until you come to the end (B).

6

Add the second section. Take the needle through the end hole immediately above, and continue sewing as before.

7

Proceed until all the sections have been sewn.

8

Then go back, filling in all the missing stitches at the head and tail. Apart from the first and last sections, all other longstitches will have double threads on the spine. You should end up back inside the first section at an end hole. Knot the two loose thread ends together and trim.

9

Turn the cover in as described on page 68-69.

japanese-style sewing

TRADITIONAL JAPANESE BINDINGS USE A STAB STITCH to bind the pages and cover together. The simplest and most elegant stitch is the four-hole or "Yotsume Toji" binding. You can use any paper in single sheets for this book, but why not try the traditional method of sewing with the folds at the fore edge. You could use a thin, delicate paper for the pages, with a rich, decorative cover chosen from the many gorgeous Japanese papers available. The sewing thread could be a contrasting color, either rich and silky or delicate and understated, but it needs to be thick enough to enhance the beauty and simplicity of the sewing pattern.

The instructions here are for a limp paper cover, select your materials from the list on page 48.

1

Fold the paper for the sections and make them square. Cut two pieces of decorative cover paper. Place one on each side of the book block. If you wish, trim the spine edge of the book before sewing.

2

Put a weight on the text block while you make the sewing holes. Lightly score a line ¾ inch in from the spine edge (A). Measure ¾ inch in from the head and tail (B). Divide the space between these two points into three, which will give you the remaining two sewing points (C). At these points, make a hole through the covers and pages using a bodkin, or needle, depending on the thickness of your book.

3

Start sewing through the spine, a few pages down from the top of the book, and come up through hole (A). Leave enough thread to tie later.

Continue sewing as shown in the diagrams.

To finish, take the needle through hole (A) and come out at the point on the spine where you started. Thread both loose ends of silk thread in the needle and take them back inside the book. If you find it difficult to match up the threads, then take the needle right up through hole (A) to the spine of the book. It may be easier to find the original sewing entrance by going back into hole (A) from here.

BACK

6

Open up the book and tie the two ends together. Trim and dab on a little glue. Close the book.

other stab stitches

IN ADDITION TO THE DECORATIVE JAPANESE SEWING described here, there are other simple forms of stab stitch that you can turn into fantastic and exotic creations.

The simplest method is to sew a continuous running stitch. Winding a colored thread through each stitch creates a whipped running stitch (A). You can oversew the spine, using very large or very small stitches, and experiment with cross-stitch (B). Try using single threads and knotting through the holes and at the spine (C). You can add tassels, beads, or driftwood, and by extending the sewing, you can create all manner of ties and wrappings (D). There really is no limit to the variations possible with this simple format.

A   B   D   C

attaching covers and

oards

THERE ARE LOTS OF WAYS YOU CAN put covers on your books once they have been sewn. In some of the sewing methods described in the previous chapter, such as the Japanese and longstitch books, the covers are attached at the time of sewing. However, the remainder of the stitches and board attachments are interchangeable, giving you the freedom to experiment with your own materials and ideas.

Tapes and cords can be glued, nailed, or sewn onto the cover boards using a variety of decorative techniques and stitches.

If you don't want the tapes to show or be part of the design, glue them between two precovered boards. Another way of attaching tapes and cords to boards is the traditional method of lacing in. This involves cutting slots or holes in the cover boards through which the sewing supports are laced. Recesses can be cut into the boards if you want the tapes or cords to lie flat. Originally, the book would have been covered after lacing, but with the exposed sewing method, the boards are usually covered first.

In addition, there are two specific projects to give you even more choice. These two books are very different in construction. One is a hardback book with pasted endpapers, and the other is a limp paper binding that requires no adhesive at all. You can use any type of paper for covering boards, but remember, the softer and more delicate the paper, the more it will wear. If you want a really tough book, use bookbinding cloth.

attaching endpapers (tipping on)

MATERIALS

Colored or decorative paper for endpapers

Waste paper

EQUIPMENT

Knife and/or scalpel

Steel safety ruler

Craft glue

Glue brush

Pressing boards and a weight

1

Cut two pieces of your chosen endpaper, and fold them in two, so that they are the same size as the pages of your book. Lay out some waste paper and place the endpapers down one on top of the other, with the folded edges about ³⁄₁₆ inch away from each other. Lay a piece of waste paper ³⁄₁₆ inch away from the top fold. Using craft glue, glue the exposed folds, brushing out to avoid getting glue underneath. Remove the waste paper and throw it away immediately.

2

Lay the book on its side, folding back the tapes. Place the glued edge of one endpaper on the top section so that the folded edge is lined up exactly with the edge of the backbone. Rub down, then turn over, and repeat with the second endpaper. Leave to dry between pressing boards under a weight. In this exposed sewing style of binding the spine is not glued, so now move onto the boards.

fill-ins

IF YOU WANT A REALLY SMOOTH, STYLISH FINISH on the inside of the cover boards, you can line them with paper before putting down the endpaper.

MATERIALS

Lining paper

Craft glue

Waxed paper

Fine sandpaper

EQUIPMENT

Knife and/or scalpel

Steel safety ruler

Cutting mat or board

Pressing boards and a weight

1

Cut two pieces of paper the same thickness as the cover paper to fit between the turn-ins on the inside of the cover boards. Make sure the grain direction runs from head to tail.

2

Coat the paper with glue and stick it down. Close the board, turn it over, and repeat on the board on the other side. Put waxed paper over the glued paper and leave to dry between pressing boards under a weight.

3

When the fill-in is dry, using a fine sandpaper, you can gently sand over the tapes, cords, etc., until the surface is smooth. Put in the endpapers as described previously.

cutting recesses

1 Cut your cover boards to the required size, adding ⅛ inch at the head, tail, and fore edge. Decide how long you want the tapes to be, then cut them to the desired length.

2 Place the boards on the book and the tapes in position, then mark the width and length of the tapes on the boards with a pair of dividers. Remove the board.

3 Using a scalpel and safety ruler, cut and peel away the area of board between the divider points to the depth of the tape.

4 Coat the boards with craft glue and cover with paper or cloth, making sure the covering material is pushed down well into the recesses. Fold, cut, and glue down the corners and turn-ins as described on pages 25–26 and leave the covered boards between waxed paper and pressing boards under a weight to dry.

MATERIALS
Cover boards
Waxed paper
Craft glue

EQUIPMENT
Knife and/or scalpel
Steel safety ruler
Cutting mat or board
Divider
Glue brush
Pressing boards and a weight

attaching boards

1 Use the equipment listed on page 60. Place the covered boards in position on the book and position the tapes over the recesses. Mark with divider points where the sewing holes are to be.

2 Remove the boards and make holes using a bodkin or small drill. Remember to use a pile of waste boards when hammering or drilling through a cover board so you don't damage the work surface.

MATERIALS

Greyboard

Cover paper or cloth

Colored or decorative
paper for endpapers

Paper for pages

Sewing thread

Mull

Kraft paper

Craft glue

Wheatflour paste

Waxed paper for
pressing

EQUIPMENT

Knife and/or scalpel

Steel safety ruler

Needle

Dividers

Cutting mat or board

Glue brushes

Drawing square

Pressing boards

3

Coat the recesses with a little craft glue and stick down the tapes. Turn over and repeat with the other side. Leave to dry between pressing boards.

4

Using your chosen sewing pattern, sew over the tapes and through the boards, knotting and gluing the thread on the inside.

5

You can either paste down the endpapers, or paste in a lining paper on the inside of the board.

i) To paste down the endpapers, put a piece of waste paper between the endpapers and paste them, brushing out from the center. Remove the waste paper and position the board squarely over the paste down (see Glossary on page 11). Turn over and repeat with the other side of the book. Place some waxed or blotting paper between the pasted endpapers and leave the book to dry thoroughly between clean paper and pressing boards under a weight.

ii) To line the boards, cut two pieces of decorative or plain lining paper ⅛ inch smaller than the board on all four sides. Apply paste and place squarely over the inside of the board. Turn over and repeat on the other side of the book.

6

Leave the book to dry as described in 5i and the book is now complete.

lacing-in boards

IF YOU NEED A STRONGER CONSTRUCTION for your book, or you want to slot the tapes or cords in and out of the boards as part of the design, you must pierce the boards as well as cut recesses.

1 Attach endpapers and cut boards to size as described previously. Decide how much of the tape or cord you want showing on the cover board. Measure but don't cut yet. Cut recesses to this measurement and cover the boards following steps 1 through 4 of Attaching Boards.

2 Using a chisel or awl, make a slit or hole at the end of each recess, where the tape or cord will go through.

3 Turn the boards over and cut recesses on the inside, extending about ¾ inch beyond the slits. If you want to weave the tapes or cords in and out of the boards, make slits and recesses accordingly.

4 Place one board in position on the book. Coat the recesses with glue, making sure a small amount goes into the slits or holes, and thread the tapes or cords through.

5 Drop the cover board back onto a pile of pressing boards. Cut the tapes or cords to fit into the recesses, glue in place, and hammer flat. Turn over and repeat on the other side of the book.

6 Put down the endpapers or lining papers as described previously and leave them to dry overnight as indicated earlier.

MATERIALS
Craft glue

EQUIPMENT
Chisel or awl
Knife and/or scalpel
Pressing boards
Hammer

case binding

THIS STYLE OF BINDING IS THE ONE we are most familiar with—the commercial hardcover book. The hard cover is referred to as a case, hence the term "case binding." It is more hardwearing than some of the more decorative structures, because the sewing is protected by spine linings and a greyboard cover. It is suitable for most uses, but especially for notebooks and sketchbooks. Check that the grain direction of all your materials runs from head to tail, especially the endpapers, or they will stretch the wrong way and buckle when pasted.

MATERIALS

Greyboard

Cover paper or cloth

Colored or decorative paper for endpapers

Paper for pages

Sewing thread

Mull

Kraft paper

Craft glue

Wheatflour paste

Waxed paper for pressing

EQUIPMENT

Knife and/or scalpel

Steel safety ruler

Needle

Dividers

Cutting mat or board

Glue brushes

Drawing square

Pressing boards

1 Sew sections onto tapes as described in Sewing on Tapes, on pages 48–49 and add endpapers as described in Attaching Endpapers, on page 58.

2 Leaving the tapes out, put the book between pressing boards and place a weight on top. Place glue along the spine, making sure you have enough glue between each of the sections by rubbing the glue in with your finger. Leave to dry.

3 If you have access to a guillotine or paper cutter with a clamp and want to trim your book, do so now.

4 Cut a piece of mull slightly shorter than the book at each end, and 1¼ to 1½ inches wider than the spine on each side. Glue the mull to the spine of the book. Don't glue the excess, this will be pasted down with the tapes later.

5

Cut two strips of kraft paper the same width as the spine, one piece to fit underneath the tapes (A), and the other to run the full length (B). Glue the small pieces to the spine first, then the full strip, and rub down well with a bone folder. If your book is large or thick, you can add an extra lining of kraft paper.

6

Cut two boards ¼ inch longer than the height of the book and ¹⁄₁₆ inch narrower than the width. Push the board out by ⅛ inch at the fore edge, giving a ³⁄₁₆ inch joint allowance. This allowance is very important—without it, the book won't open properly.

7

Place the boards in position on each side of the book and squeeze together. Measure the combined thickness of the book and both boards with dividers to determine the width of the spine board.

Note: Don't measure at the backbone. The tapes and sewing make it thicker than the rest of the book. Cut a piece of board this width, and the same height as the cover boards.

8

Cut a piece of paper or cloth ¾ inch bigger on all sides than the area of the boards and spine as laid out in the diagram. Leave more cloth or paper than you need; you can always trim it down later. Coat one board with glue and stick it down. Turn over and rub down well.

The joint allowance is ³/₁₆ inch, but you need to add a board thickness to this. Although you are gluing the spine piece down flat, when the cover is closed, it will stand on its side (A).

CLOSED

OPEN   A

Set the dividers to this measurement (A), and mark out from the edge of the glued board. Lay a ruler along the base of the board and glue the spine piece with PVA. Place in position, lining up the divider points with the edge of the spine piece, making sure that everything is level. Rub down.

A

Use the same allowance and technique to position the second board. Glue into position and rub down. Set the dividers to ⅝ inch for the turn-in, and using a scalpel and safety ruler, trim the excess paper or cloth.

Fold, crease, and cut the corners, then glue down the turn-ins as described on pages 25–26. Leave to dry under a weight between waxed paper and pressing boards.

Trim back the mull and tapes to about 1 inch using wasteboard to protect your book.

Place the book inside the case leaving an equal square all around, and pushing the book right into the spine. Lay it down flat and let the cover drop back. Put waste paper between the book and the endpaper, paste down the tapes, and then paste the whole of the endpaper, including the mull. Brush the paste from the center of the endpaper out to avoid getting paste under the endpaper. Carefully remove the waste sheet.

15

Without dislodging the book, bring the cover over, pushing the spine into the backbone of the book. Drop the cover down onto the paste down (see Glossary on page 11). Don't be tempted to open the board out flat once it is pasted, because the endpaper is wet and will stretch, causing creases when you shut the book again. Turn the book over and repeat on the other side.

Put waxed or blotting paper between the endpapers and wrap the book in clean waste paper. Place a pressing board on each side of the book as far up as the joint so the spine protrudes. Put the book in a press if you have one, or under a heavy weight. Leave the book to dry completely before use, preferably overnight. Don't use the book or leave it unweighted while the endpapers are still wet, or the boards will not dry flat.

limp paper binding
with slotted spine

THIS BOOK IS SEWN ONTO TAPES, RIBBONS, OR PAPER STRIPS that are slotted through a paper cover. There is no gluing involved, so everything is held together by folding. Once you have mastered the sewing, the rest is easy. Choose a strong, hard-wearing paper such as a handmade plant fiber or Khadi paper as illustrated in the gallery section. The sewing supports and slotted spine strip can be made from the same paper or in a contrasting color for dramatic effect. If you want something softer, you can use ribbons, which can be extended to become ties or wrappings.

MATERIALS

Strong paper for cover

Paper for pages

Ribbon, tape, or paper for sewing supports

Sewing thread

EQUIPMENT

Knife and/or scalpel

Steel safety ruler

Bone folder

Dividers

Drawing square

Cutting mat or board

Needle

1

Sew up the book as described in Sewing on Tapes.

2

Make a paper pattern for the cover. First take a sheet of paper large enough to wrap around the sewn sections with about 1¾ inches extra all around.

3

Lay the book on the paper and draw around it (A). Then turn it over, marking the spine width (B). Drop the book down and draw around the other side (C).

4

Transfer these marks to your cover paper. Extend the book edge measurements out by ⅛ inch. Score along these turn-ins and the joints with a ruler and bone folder.

6

Extend a drawn line from these points across the spine and then cut through with a sharp scalpel.

7

Cut along the spine fold between the slits and remove the paper. These holes should correspond with the position of the tapes on the book.

5

Lay the back of the book on the spine fold of the paper, and with the point of the dividers, mark the position of the tapes or ribbons.

8

Measure ⅜ inch from the top and bottom of each hole and mark with the point of the dividers (A). Cut through the cover vertically between these points (B).

9

If you are extending ribbons to make ties, cut slits along the fore edge turn-ins where desired (A) or (B).

10

Cut the cover paper as in the diagram below.

11

Cut the corners to form a tab, as shown below. The measurements are (A) = ¼ inch and (B) = ½ inch.

12

Fold all the turn-ins over along their precreased edges and mark each side of the tab with the dividers as shown.

13

Open out the folded turn-ins and make a slit between the two divider points at each corner (A).

14

Cut a spine strip from the cover paper. It should be the same height as the cover and slightly narrower than the width of the spine. Lay the spine piece in position on the cover paper and turn in the smaller tabs at (A) and (B).

15

Lay the book over the cover spine, lining up the tapes with the slits. Push each tape through the corresponding slit at the spine fold.

16

When all the tapes are pulled through, take them back inside the cover through the remaining slits. Pull tight so that the back of the book fits snugly into the spine of the cover.

17

Fold the turn-ins around the first and last pages of the book (or the endpapers if you have attached them), and push the tabs through the slots at each corner.

From left to right:

Vivien Frank's "Bestiary" uses a binding sewn in the Coptic style with no tapes. The boards are made from laminated handmade paper and the signatures are guarded with Japanese Mingei paper.

Sue Doggett's "Stab Stitch and Japanese Bindings" are made from handmade paper and silk sewing thread.

Sue Doggett and Penny Stanford's hardcover books are three case bindings (see page 62). The images on the standing books are mono-printed and colored with watercolor pencil. The cover of the book in the foreground is screen printed with text and imagery.

Sue Doggett and Vivien Frank's "Longstitch Bindings" (see page 51).

variations on the fold

ALL THE BOOKS IN THE NEXT SECTION have an accordion fold as their basic structure. In this chapter

there are all sorts of additions
to the zigzag, increasing even further the
creative possibilities of this
versatile and exciting form.

All the techniques used here have been described in detail in the previous chapter, and some of them have been developed into major projects later in the book. You don't have to stick rigidly to these instructions; you can mix and match many of the techniques to create your own formats.

Some of the bookworks use a combination of folding and sewing, and a variety of materials, so why not try some of the paper-decorating techniques described in the first chapter? All of these structures are ideal for carrying text and artwork. Perhaps you could try simple monoprinting onto a long fold of paper and then folding it into a zigzag, or use text, photocopied or made from a collage, which could be added as extra sewn-in folds, or "flags" perhaps. The gallery section has examples of all the book structures described in this chapter, with a few extras for inspiration.

accordions with sewn folds

One way of extending the fold format is to add sewn sections. This way you can make a multisection book where the accordion fold acts as a sewing support not unlike those in the previous chapters. Here, though, the support is expandable and sections can be sewn on both sides, making the format continuous. The fold of the zigzag can be narrow, like a fan fold so that the extra pages are extended, or the same size as the sections so that it works like an endpaper or cover. The former allows the pages to work as a continuous sequence with one section running into the next, while the latter breaks the sequence up.

Cover boards can be added to any of these format variations using the method described in the Pocket Fold Book.

dos-à-dos

This binding is the simplest extension of the pamphlet and zigzag combination. The fold is extended by a half-fold, and two sections are attached using the three-hole sewing method. Most structures can work in this back-to-back method, including the case binding, an example of which is illustrated in the gallery section at the end of this chapter.

Extended Dos-à-Dos

Extend the length of the zigzag fold as much as you like and add the corresponding number of sections. This example has the sewing knot outside the folds where it has been augmented and used as a decorative feature.

uneven folds

Another way of altering the format is to fold the zigzag unevenly and attach sections of varying sizes. If you want the book to stand up, emphasizing its sculptural form, you need to make sure the foot of the book is level, which sometimes means having very odd-shaped folds.

extended sections

Make a fan fold and use the pamphlet stitch to sew sections to the fold edges. This format is a great way to display prints or artwork that you want to open completely flat. If you want the book to open conventionally and have a stable spine, you can sew the accordion to sewing supports after sewing in the pages (see Multisection Sewing).

Random Sections

Sections don't have to be regularly sewn along an accordion, nor do they need to be a uniform size. The illustrated example utilizes the sculptural qualities of the folded book and experiment with the proportions between the folds and the sections. These folded books are pleasing and interesting to work with purely as forms, but they can also be used to emphasize artwork or a particular element or motif in your design.

venetian blind book

This style of binding is based on palm-leaf books made and used extensively in India and Southeast Asia. Because of their fragility, not many early versions survive, so no one knows exactly how long they have been in use for making books. There are, however, beautiful lacquered examples from the eighteenth and nineteenth century in the British Library and other collections. The long, slim palm leaves were held together by threaded strings, much like a blind, except they were all single leaves. In the Venetian blind, the strings, ribbons, or sticks are threaded through an accordion fold.

single star book

The star book, so-called for obvious reasons, has one fold of artwork per zigzag. You will need enough zigzag folds and pages to allow the book to form a complete circle. You could attach cover boards to this book, with ribbon ties to keep the book open in its star shape. See the Gallery Section on pages 80–81 for examples, or for a more complex version of the star book, see the Star Book on page 118.

flag book

THIS BOOK IS FUN AND EASY TO make. It can be read like a conventional codex by turning over page by page, but it also opens out into a panoramic sculptural form that is perfect for artwork and text. The flag book can become wonderfully architectural, if you turn it upside down and open the flags in on one another.

MATERIALS

Greyboard

Covering paper for boards and board linings

Medium-weight paper for fold and strips

Craft glue

EQUIPMENT

Knife and/or scalpel

Steel safety ruler

Cutting mat

Dividers

Bone folder

Glue brushes

Pressing boards and a weight

1 Cut two boards to the required size and cover them with your chosen paper. Allow ⅝ inch for the turn-ins, and follow the instructions as for Pocket Fold Book on page 27.

2 Cut your paper for the accordion fold to the required length (each side of the fold should be at least ¾ inch wide) and ³⁄₁₆ inch shorter than the board height. Fold the cut paper into a zigzag.

3 Glue the ends of the zigzag folds to the inside of the covered boards.

4 Cut a piece of paper for the strips ³⁄₁₆ inch shorter than the height of the zigzag fold (this allows for a small gap between the flags to avoid catching them on one another when opening the book), and ³⁄₁₆ inch narrower than the width of the boards. You will need one strip of paper for each of the folds in your zigzag book.

Decide how many flag strips you want on each of the folds and divide each page up equally.

Following the diagram below, glue the flags in position onto each of the folds. (A) and (B) strips are glued alternately on either side of the folds. Make sure you only glue about ⅜ inch on the edge of each fold to avoid any glue showing when the pages are turned conventionally.

Cut two pieces of lining paper to fit inside the boards, making sure the end of the zigzag is covered. Glue in position and leave to dry between pressing boards under a weight.

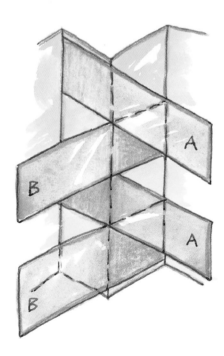

pop-up books

THIS BOOK IS BASED ON A SIMPLE FOLD and the three-hole pamphlet stitch. It contains small hidden panels that pop out when the pages are opened. The pages can be turned in sequence, or the book can stand up alone, with all the interiors on display. It could tell a story, contain a poem, or display photographs instead of the paper panels.

MATERIALS

Heavy paper or thin cardboard

Heavy paper or photographs for the panels

Sewing thread

Artwork

Craft glue

EQUIPMENT

Knife and/or scalpel

Steel safety ruler

Drawing square

Cutting mat or board

Sewing needle

Glue brush

1 Cut four pieces of cardboard or paper 4 x 10 inches and fold them each as illustrated.

(A) = 3 inches

(B) = 2⅛ inches

(C) = ⅜ inch

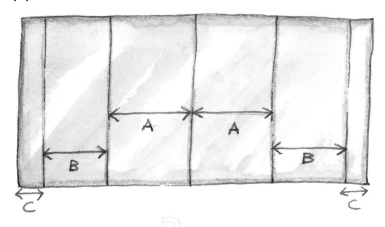

2 Cut windows, one in each of the four pages (here the window size is 1⅜ x 2⅜ inches). Then glue artwork, images, or text on the panels adjacent to the windows.

Fold two pages inside each other as pictured, then fold the two remaining pages in the same way.

Make a paper sewing pattern for three-hole sewing to fit the center fold of the pages. Make sewing holes in both sets, then sew all four pages together.

Cut four card inserts and attach image or text. If you are using the specified measurements, they should be 2⅛ x 3¾ inches. Turn the folds on the outer edges of the book in and apply glue to the insides (A). Then attach the card inserts to this glued edge.

Finally, glue the outer edge of (A) to the opposite flap and leave to dry thoroughly. To activate the pop-up, push the glued flaps toward the center of the book—the fold lines in the middle of each page will move outward to form a triangle.

INAMORATO

From left to right:

Sue Whittington and Margaret Benson's books are based on the star book format. The book in the foreground is designed using a series of cutouts and a case binding. The second book has foldout pages and is sewn onto boards covered in marbled paper.

Clare Bryan's "Alice in Wonderland" is a dos-à-dos book made from an extended case binding .

Sue Doggett's books with uneven folds and additional sections sewn in, can extend the accordion fold in as many directions as you want.

Sue Doggett's "Inamorato" is a bookwork made from the star book format, using photocopied acetates, collage, copper wire, handmade paper pulp, and dried lilies.

Helen Hutchins and Penny Stanford's "Accordion Books" show how wooden pages offer an alternative tactile experience (below left), and by printing on both sides of the accordion fold, the text and image can work as a continuous story line (below right).

containers

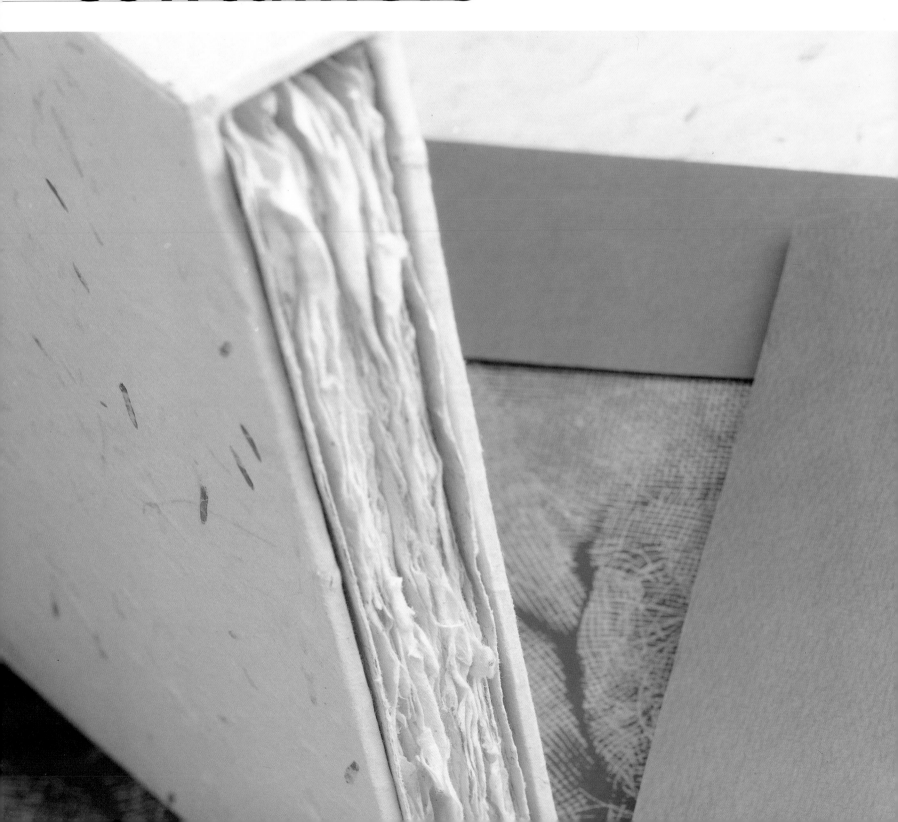

BOXES AND PORTFOLIOS ARE IDEAL for storing papers and objects, or protecting precious books. Even when storing serious contents, boxes needn't be dull and boring.

They can be both beautiful and hard wearing, **perfect for anything** from account books to gift boxes.

If the container is for important documents, choose more durable materials, such as bookbinding cloth. Cloth comes in a variety of colors that can be embellished using decorative papers, ties, and ribbons. For a sharp, stylish finish, try using eyelet fastenings or toggles. The two projects described in this chapter are a simple portfolio and a slipcase. This introduction teaches some basic techniques, and there is a Japanese-style wraparound case for you to experiment with later.

portfolio

THIS PORTFOLIO IS MADE FROM TWO BOARDS hinged with a cloth spine and covered with decorative paper. Inside are three flaps made from thick paper, which are creased and folded around your documents, notes, or artwork to keep them safe. The width of the spine will determine the storage capacity of the folio, and the flaps can be folded to match.

MATERIALS

Cover board

Bookcloth for the spine

Thick paper for flaps

Paper for lining and
covering boards

Ribbon or tape for ties

Craft glue

Wheatflour paste

EQUIPMENT

Knife and/or scalpel

Dividers

Bone folder

Pencil

Steel safety ruler

Chisel and hammer

Cutting mat

Pressing boards

1

Cut two boards to your chosen size (ours is 9 x 12 inches) with the grain direction running from head to tail.

2

To make the cloth spine piece, first decide how deep you want the portfolio to be (A). To this measurement add 4 inches (B). This should be the width of the cloth. The length will be the height of the boards plus 1½ inches (C). Cut the cloth to size.

3

Set the dividers to 2 inches and score lengthwise along the edge of both boards (A). Apply glue to this area and lay the cloth down, lining it up with the scored line. Rub down well and then repeat on the other board.

4

Trim the turn-ins to ⅝ inch, coat with glue, and turn them over the board edges. Rub down.

6

Cut two pieces of cover paper to overlap the spine cloth by ⅛ inch (A) and to extend ¾ inch past the board on the other three edges (B).

5

Cut another piece of bookcloth for the spine lining. This should be the same height as the boards and the width of the original spine piece. Coat the cloth with glue and stick it to the inside of the spine. Make sure you work the cloth into the board edges and rub down well across the spine.

7

To avoid getting any glue on the cloth, coat the board with glue as far as the cloth edge, then run a little glue along the inside edge of the cover paper. Place the paper on the glued board, overlapping the cloth by ⅛ inch, and rub down well.

8

Trim the turn-ins to ⅝ inch using a scalpel and safety ruler and fold, crease, and cut the corners as illustrated.

9

Now glue the turn-ins as before and leave the portfolio to dry under a weight between waxed or clean paper and pressing boards.

10

Cut two lengths of ribbon or tape for the ties, approximately 4 inches long each. Find the center of the board height and make a pencil mark ¾ inch in from the board edge at this point. Using a knife or a hammer and chisel, make a slit over this point wide enough for the ribbon. Repeat on the other board so that the two slits are exactly opposite each other.

11

Pull the ribbons through the board (A), secure with glue, and hammer flat (B).

12

For the flaps, cut three pieces of heavy paper the same width as the spine allowance (between the boards) (B), adding ¾ inch for turn-ins (A) and 2¼ to 3¼ inches for the folds (C) depending on the size of the portfolio. One of the pieces should be cut to the length of the board, and the other two should be equal to the width. Score the above measurements onto the paper and crease. The inner corners of the turn-ins can be mitered for a neater finish (see (D) below). Trim the flap edges as shown at (E) and make a zigzag by folding section (F) in half.

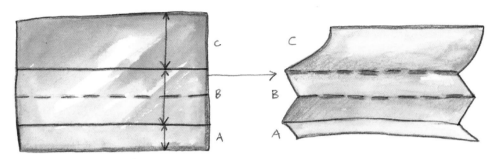

14

Cut two pieces of lining paper (with the grain direction running head to tail) to fit inside the boards. Measure the inside edges of the boards and cut the lining paper about ⅛ inch narrower all around.

Paste the paper in position and rub down. Leave to dry overnight in the usual way. If you have large pressing boards, it is better to open out the portfolio and let it dry completely flat. It is also a good idea to leave the flaps and ribbons folded out when drying to avoid any unwanted indentations in the portfolio.

13

Coat the turn-ins of each flap with glue and place them on the right-hand board, lining the creased edge up with the edge of the board. Rub down well.

slipcase

A SLIPCASE FORMS A STRONG PROTECTIVE BOX for your books, and it can be covered in paper or cloth. The boards are lined before the box is assembled, which makes the construction simple. The most important thing here is accuracy, and rather than calculating lots of small measurements, it is probably easier to use the dividers.

MATERIALS

Greyboard

Cover paper or bookcloth

Lining paper

Craft glue

Masking tape

Medium-grit sandpaper

EQUIPMENT

Knife and/or scalpel

Bone folder

Steel safety ruler

Dividers

Glue brush

Small stiff paintbrush

Drawing square

Pressing boards

Sanding block

1 Cover a piece of greyboard with your chosen lining paper using glue. Rub it down well through clean paper and leave it to dry between pressing boards under a weight. To estimate the amount of paper needed, measure twice the height of the book and add on 2 inches (A), and the width plus twice the thickness of the book adding 2 to 2¼ inches (B).

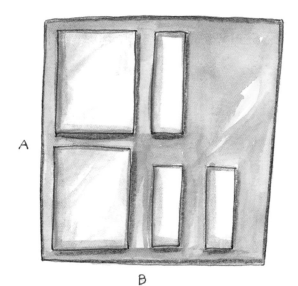

2 Measure the book for the slipcase from head to tail (A) and from spine to fore edge (B). Also measure the thickness (C).

Cut the boards to size from the lined greyboard, following the measurements below. Make your measurements with the dividers.

1) Box sides (cut two)

(A) Height = height of book plus 2 board thicknesses plus 2 thicknesses of covering material

(B) Width = width of book plus 1 board thickness

2) Long wall (cut one)

(C) Height = same as height of box side

(D) Width = thickness of book plus 2 thicknesses of covering material

3) Short walls (cut two)

(E) Length = same as width of box side minus 1 board thickness

(F) Width = same as width of long wall

Cut or tear masking tape into lots of small pieces. Then, using a stiff paintbrush, apply glue to the edge of the long wall. Attach the long wall to one of the box sides and stick pieces of masking tape around the jointed boards.

Coat the edges of one of the short walls with glue, and attach it to the box side in the same way. Repeat with the remaining short wall.

Coat the exposed edges of the walls already in place with glue, and attach the second box side. When all the glue is dry, remove the masking tape carefully.

Any unevenness or rough edges will show through the paper or cloth, so use medium-grit sandpaper and a sanding block to smooth the board edges before covering.

Cut enough paper to cover the box as follows:

(A) = depth of box and (B) = ¾ inch.

Coat one side of the box with glue and apply your covering material, leaving ¾ inch for the turn-in. Rub down well before moving to the next stage. Then coat the spine of the box with glue and fold the covering material around, making sure you have no air bubbles at the joint. Rub down well. Finally, coat the second box side with glue and wrap the material around it, rubbing down as before.

Crease the covering material where it folds around the spine (A). Trim the spine turn-in back to ⅜ inch, angle the corners, and glue down. Repeat at the other end.

Cut one of the flaps of paper at the end of the box to fit the width of the short wall. Coat with glue and stick down, then trim the turn-in (A) back to the board edge at the open end of the box. Repeat at the other end.

11

Cut the remaining two flaps of covering material to fit the width of the short wall, glue, and rub down well. This time, do not trim at the open end of the box. Repeat at the other end.

12

Crease the material from the corners of the box (A) at the open end and cut along this line. Then measure one board thickness away from this cut on each side (B) and (C) and make a cut along that line. Repeat on all four corners.

13

Cut the small tabs in each corner to ¼ inch and glue down as illustrated.

14

Coat the turn-ins with glue and fold them over the board edges, rubbing down well.

15

Leave the box to dry before slipping your book in it.

From left to right:

Clare Bryan's "Open-Closed Box" shows accordion folds enclosed in a CD case and then slotted into a slipcase made from printed greyboard.

Clare Bryan's "Open-Closed Books" are made from accordion fold books using drawing paper and color photocopies, and brass eyelets.

Helen Hutchins' "Three Books and Slipcase" are each case bound, single-section books with marbled paper covers in a slipcase.

Emma Ruffle's Japanese-style wraparound case has carved wooden toggles and printed Japanese paper linings.

Sue Doggett's "Mr. Palomar Case" consists of three screen printed books in a wooden case with compartmants and a sliding glass door.

the projects

SO FAR YOU HAVE EXPERIENCED A NUMBER of different book structures and formats, and some basic techniques for making them.

The next section consists of ten specific projects, ## described step-by-step, ### which will utilize and develop these techniques.

Some new approaches have been added, including elements of design and new formats with which you can experiment. Although the projects are given titles, such as diary or journal, most of them are interchangeable. A sketchbook could be an album, and an album could be a diary, for example. The size of each model is given at the beginning of each project, and the measurements in the instructions apply to a book of this size. Of course, you can change the scale, materials, and sometimes even the sewing techniques to make your own version of each structure, but it is probably a good idea to make a test piece first since the proportions will change.

All the projects in this section use greyboard that is approximately $\frac{3}{16}$ inch thick, except the Poem Book and Rebinding a Book, which are made from a thinner $\frac{1}{8}$-inch board. Where techniques are repeated, you will be referred to the relevant section in the first half of the book or to the gallery sections for inspiration and other examples of a specified project. Create your own beautiful bookworks by drawing upon any of the techniques you have already experienced, and all the new ideas you will want to experiment with from this section.

photograph album

an album is one of the most popular ways of
storing and displaying memorabilia such as
photographs, postcards, tickets,
and so on, but it can also be used as a visitors' book, journal, or sketchbook.
The beauty of this structure is that it is expandable—you can add more pages when you need them.

The brass screw posts used to hold the binding together can be bought in various sizes so

that you can make your album exactly the thickness you want, and if you change your mind,

just add an extension post or two. The

model pictured is made using alternating

black and white pages, and the boards are

covered in a three-color paste paper. The

method for making paste papers is described

in the section on materials at the beginning

of the book. The spine boards are covered in

bookcloth which is extended to become a

strong, flexible hinge.

**The size of the model pictured is
9⅛ x 6¾ x 1 inches**

1

Cut the paper for the pages to the required size adding on an extra ¾ inch for the guards (A). Guards allow for the extra thickness of your mounted photographs or scraps, to stop the book from becoming wedge-shaped. Mark ¾ inch in from the edge of the paper with the dividers. Using a steel ruler and bone folder, crease along the divider points and fold. Repeat for every page to form the guards.

2

With the guards folded over, place pages inside each other as shown.

3

To determine the size of the brass posts, measure the total thickness of the folded pages (including the folded guards) and add roughly ¼ inch to allow for the lined cover boards (A).

4

Cut two boards ⅛ inch larger than the folded pages on all four sides. Measure 1 inch in from the edge of each board and cut off (A); these are the spine boards. Then trim ³⁄₁₆ inch off the width of the larger boards. This gives you the joint allowance (B).

5

Measure the height of a spine board and divide into three (A). Then measure ½ inch in from the long edge (B). These are the two points at which to drill holes for the brass posts.

MATERIALS

Paper for pages, fairly heavy if you want to mount photographs

Greyboard

Decorative or colored cover paper

Bookcloth for the spine and hinge

Paper for lining the boards inside

Brass posts and extensions

Craft glue

Wheatflour paste

Waxed paper

EQUIPMENT

Knife and/or scalpel

Steel safety ruler

Cutting mat or board

Dividers

Bone folder

Glue and paste brushes

C-clamps

Hand drill (or hole punch)

Pressing boards

6

Clamp the two spine boards together with the C-clamps over a pile of spare board. Put the spine board on which you marked the hole placement on top. Make two holes through the spine boards using a hand drill. If you use a hole punch, you will need to mark both boards and make the holes individually.

Stack your book sections, align them squarely at the folded edge, and place on top of a pile of spare board. Cut a piece of greyboard the height of the folds and approximately 2 inches wide (A). Lay this board on the folded edge of the book (B). Place one of the drilled spine boards over the book and greyboard, allowing for the ⅛-inch square (C). Transfer the position of the holes from the spine board to the waste greyboard (A).

8

Remove the spine board and clamp the book and spare board in position at each end as before. Drill through. It is more difficult to use a hole punch for this job, but it can be done if you are accurate and careful. To do this, mark one section and punch out the holes. Then place it squarely on the next section and either mark where the holes are, or punch straight through. Continue, using the first section as a guide, until all sections are complete.

To cover the spine boards, cut two pieces of bookcloth larger than you need. Glue the boards to the cloth and trim the bookcloth to size, allowing ½-inch turn-in (B) on three edges and 1³⁄₁₆ inches on the other (A), which will form the hinge.

Cut the two corners at the spine edge, then turn over and glue as described in the Pocket Fold Book, on page 26.

Glue your chosen cover paper to the back and front boards, leaving a turn-in allowance of ⅝ inch. Cut the corners of one of the short edges on each board as shown in the diagram (A) and glue it down onto the board. Do not turn in the other edges yet.

Glue the covered edge of the boards to the hinge cloth, leaving a ³⁄₁₆-inch joint allowance (A). Trim the corners as before (B) and glue down the turn-ins. Leave to dry between waxed paper and pressing boards.

Cut two pieces of lining paper (with the grain direction running from head to tail) ⅛ inch smaller than the cover boards on all four edges. Coat the papers with wheatflour paste and place in position. Rub down well, making sure the paper is worked into the joint. Leave to dry under a weight between waxed paper or blotting paper and pressing boards.

Punch or cut through the lining paper and bookcloth over the drilled holes, and place the pages between the cover boards and insert the brass posts.

journal

this simple binding is ideal for daily or
occasional writing and personal notes,
but as with many of the other structures described here,
it can be used as a sketchbook or album just as effectively.

The cutout panel in the front board allows you to create a combined cover design and title page. The small image used on the front of this model is a linoleum block print made using water-based printing ink and handpainted with watercolors. The image is mounted on a piece of Mexican bark paper that forms a visual link between the color of the pages and the cover paper. The binding is elegant and easy to make using eyelets and a silk cord. Like the photograph album, this book can also be extended because there is no adhesive on the spine.

The size of the journal pictured here is 7 x 10¼ inches.

1

Cut and fold paper for the pages to size. This model has four sections of four pages, but you can use more. With dividers, mark in ¾ inch from the folded edge of each section, and using a bone folder and ruler, score and crease along these points (A).

2

Measure the height of the book and divide into three. Punch or drill holes at the two points (A and B) through each section.

3

Cut two cover boards ⅛ inch larger than the book all around. Using one section as a pattern, transfer the position of the holes to both boards, and punch them out.

4

Measure ¾ inch in from the spine edge of the board (where you have just punched the holes) and cut this strip away (A). Repeat with the other board, then put the spine strips to one side.

5

Trim away ³⁄₁₆ inch from the edge of the two larger pieces of board (A) to produce the joint allowance.

MATERIALS

Greyboard

Cover paper

Eyelets

Paper for pages

Lining paper

Waxed paper for pressing

Cord for binding

Print, drawing, photograph, etc., for front cover

Masking tape

Craft glue and wheatflour paste

EQUIPMENT

Knife and/or scalpel

Cutting mat or board

Steel safety ruler

Bone folder

Dividers

Paste brushes

Eyelet punch

Pressing boards and a weight

6

Mount your chosen image on a piece of decorative paper and trim to size (here it is 1¾ x 2 inches)

7

To cut the window in the front board, find the center point by dividing the board in half lengthwise and widthwise (A and B). Measure ⅜ inch up from the center line (C), position your artwork, and add ³⁄₁₆ inch to each edge. Cut out the area inside this border.

8

Cut two strips of bookcloth, 1¼ inches wide and the height of the boards, and attach one edge of each strip to each of the spine strips with glue.

9

Mark two points on the cloth ³⁄₁₆ inch away from the edge of the spine piece (A). Coat the inside edge of the cover board with glue and attach to the cloth (B).

10

Cut four tiny strips of cover paper ⅛ x ⁵⁄₁₆ inch and glue them around the inner corners of the window on the front board.

11

Cut two pieces of cover paper approximately ¾ inch larger than the boards on all four sides. Coat the boards with glue and apply the paper, rubbing down well into the joints through a piece of clean paper. Trim the turn-ins to ⅝ inch, fold and cut the corners as usual, and glue down the turn-ins. Leave the boards to dry under a weight between clean or waxed paper and pressing boards.

12

To turn in the cover paper at the window, trim the paper as illustrated, cutting diagonally into each corner. Trim the turn-ins to ⅝ inch and glue down. Using a bone folder, carefully work the paper into the corners of the window. When the glue is dry, trim the turn-ins on the inside of the boards back to ⅛ inch for neatness.

13

Cut two pieces of lining paper ⅛ inch smaller than the boards on all four edges. Place one of the linings in position on the front board and anchor it temporarily with masking tape. Turn the board over and transfer the size of the cutout to the lining paper by scoring around the edge of the window with a bone folder. Remove the paper from the board and peel off the masking tape.

14

Cut out the square from the lining paper, taking away an extra ¹⁄₁₆ inch to allow for the thickness of the cover paper. Coat the lining papers with wheatflour paste, position them on the boards, and rub down. Press, then leave under a weight between waxed or blotting paper and pressing boards to dry.

15

Cut through the paper covering the punched holes and work the excess into the recesses, then press in the eyelets using an eyelet punch.

16

Paste your artwork into position on the front page of your book and leave to dry under a weight between waxed paper and pressing boards.

17

To finish your journal, take the cord through the eyelets as illustrated in the diagram, knotting both ends to prevent them from fraying.

scrapbook

this binding was made using a variety of handmade papers with just a hint of color to bring out the warmth of the natural materials. The ties are made from hemp cord knotted and embellished with a broken necklace from Thailand and a few wooden beads, and the clasp is made from a piece of driftwood found on a beach in Wales.

A scrapbook can contain papers of considerable thickness, as long as it has corresponding guards at the spine to accommodate the extra thickness, and stop the book becoming wedge-shaped. The guards in this model are made from Indian silk paper and scraps of the cover paper. The guards are torn instead of cut, which gives them a softer appearance more in keeping with the feel of the book.

The size of the scrapbook pictured here is 9½ x 6¾ x ⅜ inches.

1

Fold the paper for the pages. Tear the guards to size, and place a guard (or two if the papers are very thin) between each fold of paper. Assemble into sections.

2

Sew the sections to cords or thongs following steps 1 through 3 of Sewing over Cords or Thongs, using matching sewing thread.

3

Cut two boards ⅛ inch larger than the pages at the head, foot, and fore edge. Mark the boards for lacing in the cords and cut recesses on the front and back of the board as described in steps 1 through 4 of Cutting Recesses. Cover the boards, cutting and gluing corners and turn-ins as described in steps 4 through 8 of the Pocket Fold Book.

4

Lace on your covered boards as described in steps 2 through 5 of Lacing-in Boards.

MATERIALS

Greyboard

Paper for pages

Paper for guards

Endpapers

Cover paper

Cord, string, or waxed linen thread

A selection of beads

Driftwood or thin doweling

Matching sewing thread

Colored thread for attaching ties

Craft glue

Wheatflour paste

Waxed paper for pressing

EQUIPMENT

Knife and/or scalpel

Cutting mat or board

Bone folder

C-clamps

Dividers

Glue and paste brushes

Bodkin

Sewing needle

Small drill

Pressing boards and a weight

5

Make the clasp by drilling two holes through the driftwood or doweling with a small drill. You will need to clamp the wood down to hold it in position, and remember to use plenty of spare boards to protect your work surface.

6

Make two ties, five times the width of the book, from twine, cord, threads, or string, and tie one at each end of the clasp (A). Then take the two ties to the back cover board and mark sewing positions (B).

7

Drill or use a bodkin to make the sewing holes through the cover board.

8

Attach the ties with stitching of your choice, using colored thread. You may need to sew through, as well as over, the ties since they may slide around.

Wrap the ties around the book, knotting and beading the cords as you go. When you are happy with how the ties look, unwrap them.

10

The next step is filling-in, which is optional and can be applied to many projects in this book. Filling in gives a stylish finish to the insides of the boards and allows you to remove lumps and bumps caused by lacing-in and sewing. To make fillers, see Attaching Boards and follow steps 1 through 3 of Fill-ins.

Cut the endpapers the same size as the pages of the book. Paste them down with wheatflour paste and put a sheet of waxed or blotting paper between them. Then put a piece of thick, protective paper (with a torn edge) under the ties on the back board to avoid any unwanted impressions. Put the book under a weight between waxed paper and pressing boards to dry overnight. When the endpapers are dry, the book can be tied, and the cords wrapped around the wooden clasp.

four books in a box

japanese sewing techniques are among the most decorative to work,
and you have already seen the four-hole pattern
on page 53. Here, the project has been extended to include three
other methods of sewing and a wraparound box.

The papers used in the models are a mixture of Japanese and handmade Indian varieties, and they are sewn together with contrasting embroidery thread. To tear the paper in a straight line, wet it first with a damp paint brush against a ruler to release the fibers and give you a mock deckled edge. The collage design is applied with wheatflour paste. The sewing patterns need to be accurate to look good, so you must be careful when placing the holes. Using the same proportions for each of the books and scoring the base line of each pattern with a bone folder will help you achieve a perfect finish. The wraparound box is simple to make and can be covered in cloth or paper and fastened with ribbon, toggles, or twisted threads. In this example, an element of the book design is repeated on the cover.

**The books pictured are 3¾ x 7½ x ⅛ inches.
The box is 4 x 8 x ¾ inches.**

Make the pages and cover as described in Japanese-style Sewing on page 53. If you are going to add artwork or include torn and folded pages, do this before any sewing so the paste can dry thoroughly. Leave pasted papers to dry between sheets of blotting paper under weighted pressing boards.

Follow steps 2 through 6 of Japanese-Style Sewing to complete the sewing pattern for Yotsume Toji (four-hole binding).

Make sewing holes in the other three books as illustrated. (A) is called Kangxi Toji (noble binding), (B) is Asa-no-ha Toji (hemp-leaf binding), and (C) is called Kikko Toji (tortoiseshell binding).

To sew the Kangxi Toji pattern, work as the Yotsume Toji to the corners, then take threads through the extra sewing hole as illustrated.

MATERIALS
Paper for pages and cover

Embroidery thread

Greyboard

Cloth or paper for box covering

Heavy paper for box side wraps

Craft glue

Wheatflour paste for collage (optional)

Threads, ribbon, etc., for ties

Blotting paper

Waxed paper

EQUIPMENT
Knife and/or scalpel

Cutting mat or board

Steel safety ruler

Bone folder

Dividers

Sewing needle

Glue brush

Hammer

Pressing boards and a weight

5

To work the sewing patterns of Asa-no-ha Toji, follow the instructions for Kangxi Toji and then proceed as shown in the diagrams. Finish off in the usual way.

6

The pattern for Kikko Toji is worked in figures of three stitches as illustrated. Finish off as before.

7

Place the books on top of one another and measure head to tail, spine to fore edge, and their combined thickness. The sizes of the boards for the box should be as follows (all boards are the same height):

(A) Inner lid   = Spine to fore edge of the books

(B) Base   = (A) plus one board thickness

(C) Outer lid   = (A) plus two board thicknesses

(D) Spine wall   = Combined thickness of all four books

(E) Fore edge wall = (D) plus one board thickness

(F) Height   = Height of the books plus two board thicknesses

Cut the boards with the grain direction running from head to tail.

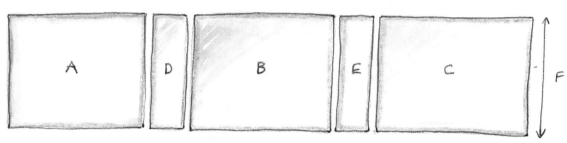

8

Cut the covering material slightly larger all around than the boards and glue each board down on it as shown, leaving a ⅛-inch gap between each piece. Rub down well. Trim the turn-ins to ¾ inch, cut the corners as usual, and glue down each of the four sides. Leave to dry under a weight between waxed paper and pressing boards.

9

Cut two pieces of heavy paper for the top and bottom wraps that hold the books in place. These should be slightly narrower than the width of the box base (A) and the same height (B), plus the combined thickness of the books (C) and a ¾ inch turn-in allowance (D). Using a bone folder and ruler, crease along these lines.

Coat the turn-in allowance with glue and attach to the head and tail of the box base. The wraps can be shaped if you prefer.

On the outside, make slits or holes (depending on your method of fastening) ⅜ inch in from the edge of the outer board, either one in the center or two—one at the head and tail (A). Then make corresponding slits or holes in the center of the spine wall (B). Thread the ties through and glue to the inside of the boards. Hammer flat.

Cut two pieces of covering material to line the spine and fore edge walls. The length is ¼ inch shorter than the height of the box and the width is that of the spine or fore edge wall plus 1⅜ inches. The corners can be cut to a 45-degree angle if desired. Glue and position over the two walls, rubbing down well into the joints.

13

Cut three pieces of lining paper to cover the inside of the boards, ⅛ inch smaller than the boards on all four sides. Fold the top and bottom wraps to the front so that they do not get any glue on them. Then coat the linings with paste or glue and attach them to the boards. Rub down well through clean paper and leave to dry under a weight between waxed or blotting paper and pressing boards.

theater book

this book form is reminiscent of a toy theater
and is also called a tunnel book because of its telescopic nature.
There are many applications for this unusual format.
It can be closed to form a three-dimensional picture or opened out
to become a theater set for your own production.

The artwork in this model is a collage made from a variety of materials—torn paper,

watercolor pencils, and altered photocopies—and is based loosely on a vacation in Italy. You

could use family photographs to make an

unusual portrait, or reduce the scale to form

a fantasy greeting card or storybook. The

structure is based around two accordion

folds that support a series of panels.

**The theater book pictured here is
10¼ x 8¼ x 8¼ inches fully extended.**

1

Decide on your imagery or design and gather together all the collage materials you need. Make the panels, starting with the back one, (shown here as sky), which is full size. Add an extra ¾ inch to the width of each panel, except the back one (A), to form tabs. These form a hinge which will attach the artwork to the side accordion folds of the book. The pictured model has five panels including the back one; it is probably best to limit the number during your initial experimentation so that the image doesn't become too complicated. Before cutting, glue all your artwork to thin cardboard and leave between pressing boards to dry.

2

Working forward from the back to the front, cut each panel smaller as you work toward the front of the book. Since the panels are of different heights, you will need to cut your tabs accordingly. If you wish, you can round off the top edge of the tab for a neat finish (A). Fold back along the edge of each panel.

MATERIALS

Greyboard

Thin cardboard for mounting artwork

Photographs, artwork, collage materials, etc., for the panels

Heavy paper for the accordion folds

Craft glue

Paint, colored pencils, etc., if desired

EQUIPMENT

Knife and/or scalpel

Steel safety ruler

Cutting mat or board

Dividers

Bone folder

Glue brushes

Paint brushes (optional)

Pressing boards

3

Fold two accordions for the side wings, the same height as the back panel (A). In the model, each fold measures 2 inches (B). If you are making a smaller book, reduce the width a little to give it visual balance. You will need one fold for each panel, not including the back one.

4

Glue the panels to one of the folded side wings as shown. Repeat with the second folded side wing and leave folded between pressing boards to dry.

Apply glue to the half-fold of each accordion panel at the back (A), and attach them to the last panel that forms the backdrop (B).

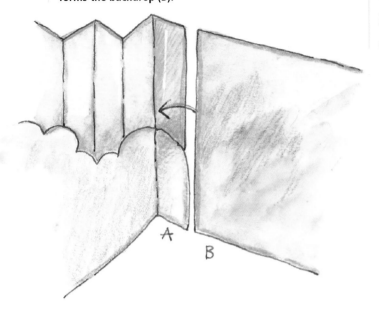

If your front board has sides which are narrower than the fold you will need to trim the accordion folds to fit (A). Apply glue to the trimmed half-folds and attach the front board, rubbing down well. Leave between waxed paper and pressing boards to dry.

To finish the front of the book, cut a piece of greyboard the same size as the back panel (A). Cut out a central area, which allows you to see all your artwork (B). The board in the model is covered with corrugated paper to give the impression of curtains. This paper is cut flush with the edge of the board, which has been painted a contrasting color.

Here the inside of the board has been shaped slightly. You can cut yours to whatever design suits the theme of your book. It can even be a continuation of the image.

star book

this version of the star book is based on a triple accordion fold and is a fun format for cards, storybooks, or poems. **It can be read coventionally by turning over one page at a time or displayed in its sculptural form, which makes it ideal for artwork.**

The example below is an imaginary planetary landscape with shooting stars made from foam rubber. The main composition of the book is made using a collage of handmade paper, photocopies, copper wire, and watercolors. Each fold is a different width, so the images become three-dimensional, with the smallest at the front and the largest at the back. They are held in place by a pamphlet stitch at the front fold and are protected by two covered boards. Have a look in the gallery sections for other interpretations of this format and then let your own imagination run wild. The possibilities for fantastic landscapes and interiors are limitless.

The size of the book shown here is 4⅜ x 5⅛ x 1⅛ inches when closed and approximately 33½ inches long when fully extended.

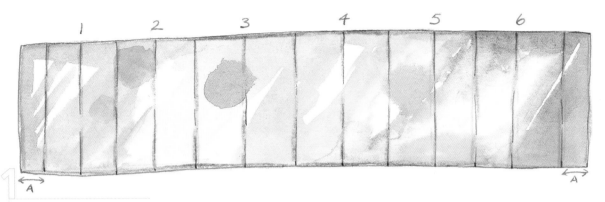

1 Design and make three panels. Start with the background. Decide on the number of folds you want. Here it is six, with the width of each page (half a fold) measuring 4⅛ inches. Allow an extra 1 inch at each end of your length of paper, which will be attached to the boards (A). You could have cutouts in this back fold, but it must remain strong enough to support the other, more fragile folds. Fold into an accordion as described in the chapter on folding.

2 Next, design and make the other two panels which relate visually to the background wall. You need the same number of folds as before, but this time they are gradated in size. The width of each page on the front fold is 2¾ inches, while the pages of the central fold are 3⅜ inches in width. Fold the accordion pleats to size, keeping in mind that the difference in size between the back (A) and middle (B) folds should be greater than between the middle and front (C) folds. Before the pictured model was sewn together, the edges of each fold were painted with acrylic paint to emphasize the star shape and hide all traces of the white paper.

3 Make a sewing pattern as described in Pamphlet Sewing, using the height of the fold to calculate the sewing points. Put all three folds of paper together and using a needle, make the holes for sewing.

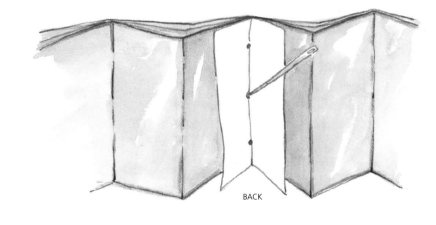

BACK

A
B
C

MATERIALS
Materials for collage and artwork
Heavy paper for the folds
Colored thread (waxed)
Greyboard
Thin cardboard
Cover paper or bookcloth
Waxed paper
Craft glue

EQUIPMENT
Knife and/or scalpel
Dividers
Cutting mat or board
Bone folder
Glue brush
Sewing needle

4

Sew the book together. The knots can be hidden or used as part of the design so you can choose to have them at the front or the back.

6

Cut two boards ¹⁄₁₆ inch larger than the book on all four sides and cover with paper or cloth, turning in only one of the long edges (A).

5

Glue each of the 1-inch folds together (A), rubbing them down well.

7

Measure the thickness of the small folds with the dividers and find a piece of thin cardboard to match and act as a filler.

8

Apply glue to the back of the small folds and attach them to the covered edge of the boards, inside the $\frac{1}{16}$ inch allowance made in step 6.

9

Cut two pieces of the filler cardboard to fit the area between the board edges and the small fold at both ends. Glue in position and leave under a weight to dry.

10

Trim the remaining turn-ins to $\frac{5}{8}$ inch, cut the corners, and glue them down.

11

Cut two pieces of lining paper to fit the inside of the boards. Paste down and leave to dry under weighted boards between sheets of waxed or blotting paper.

diary with a clasp

a clasp inspired by medieval jewelry and richly painted endpapers
will turn a standard case-binding
into a personal, gothic-style book of hours
that you will enjoy writing in every day.

The clasp itself is made from twisted copper wire and upholstery tacks (with most of the pin cut off) on a base of thin cardboard, and the strap is made from two layers of bookcloth painted the same colors as the clasp. The back of the clasp and strap are then lined with felt and attached to the board with glue and silk and thread. An extension to the design is embossed on the cover board using shaped scraps of greyboard. Of course, you can experiment with brass or silver wire, colored glass, or old pieces of jewelry; and the design of the clasp can be simple and elegant with just a few twists of wire, or highly wrought like this one.

**The size of this diary is
6¾ x 6 x ⅝ inches.**

1

Fold, cut, press, and sew the pages of the diary as described in Sewing on Tapes, on pages 48–49.

2

For the clasp cut two pieces of thin cardboard to your desired shape and decide upon the width of the strap, (here ¾ inch). Cut two pieces of cloth twice this width and approximately 4 inches long, then glue them together. Fold both edges around to meet in the center; crease and glue down. Press for a couple of minutes.

3

Glue the strap to one of the cardboard shapes made in step 2 (A). Then cut another piece of thin cardboard the same size as (A), but cut to fit around the end of the strap (B). Glue this down. Finally glue the second cardboard shape over the top of (B) so the strap is sandwiched between (C).

4

Cover the clasp with glued, crumpled paper and wind the wire around and through the shaped board, adding upholstery tacks or whatever you have chosen to use. Paint the clasp and strap with acrylics, then wipe it from the wire. Continue painting and wiping until you have achieved the effect you want.

5

Glue a piece of oversized felt to the back of the clasp and strap, and when the glue is dry, trim the felt to size. Put to one side.

MATERIALS

Greyboard

Bookcloth

Paper for pages

Decorated endpapers

Linen sewing thread

Mull

Kraft paper

Thin cardboard

Materials for clasp

Acrylic paints

Copper wire

Felt to match or contrast with the bookcloth

Waxed paper

Craft glue

Wheatflour paste

Matching touch-and-close fastening

EQUIPMENT

Knife and/or scalpel

Steel safety ruler

Cutting mat or board

Bone folder

Dividers

Glue and paste brushes

Sewing needle

Wire cutters and pliers (optional)

A piece of thick foam, bigger than the size of the cover boards

Press or pressing boards and C-clamps

Hammer (and chisel, optional)

6

Make a pair of decorative endpapers using one of the techniques described in the Paper Section or use commercially printed papers and attach them to the book as described in Attaching Endpapers, page 58. To glue the spine, trim the book (if preferred), line the spine, and cut the cover boards, follow steps 2 through 7 of the Case Binding project on pages 62–63.

7

Before gluing on the second board, you need to add the cutout shape that forms the raised area. Using the clasp as a pattern, extend the design onto a piece of thin cardboard and cut it out. Glue this shape in position on the front board.

8

So that the strap sits securely and neatly on the back board, it is advisable to cut a recess in the board. To do this, mark the center point of the long edge of the board (A) and position the strap so that the center of it lines up with point (A). Add just under ⅛ inch on each side of the strap and mark with a couple of divider points (B). The recess on the model is 1¾ inches long, but you can make it longer or slightly shorter, if you wish (C).

9

Measure the thickness of the strap with the dividers and cut the same thickness of board out of the recess. Using a strong knife, or a hammer and chisel, cut through at point (A) and cut the recess as marked in step 8.

10

Turn the board over and make another recess the same width as before and 1 inch long, toward the spine edge, away from the slit (A).

Cut your covering cloth ¾ inch bigger all around than the area of the boards and spine. Use steps 8 through 12 in the Case Binding project on pages 63–64, but this time, the cover boards need to be pressed as you glue them. If you don't have a press, use pressing boards and two C-clamps. When you have applied the cloth, place the cover board cloth side up on a pressing board (A), lay the foam over the top (B) and cover it with another pressing board (C). Place in the press or between two clamps and tighten until the foam is almost flat. Leave for 10 to 15 minutes. Do this on both front and back boards, attaching the spine piece in the center, and leave it to dry under a weight between waxed paper and pressing boards.

Place the pages of the diary, prepared in step 1, in the completed case and measure the required length of the strap. This will be from (A) through (B) to (C) in the diagram. Place the clasp in position, take the strap around the fore edge of the book and through the slit at (B). Cut the strap to fit into the inner recess, glue, and hammer flat.

Glue the strap into the recess on the outside of the board. If you wish, you can add decorative stitches made from silk thread or painted twine, taking them through the board and recessing them on the inside of the board.

Trim the mull and the tapes to an equal length and put down the endpapers as in steps 14 through 16 of the Case Binding project on page 65. Make sure you press the book with the strap undone using the foam, or you won't get an even pressing.

The next day, when the book is thoroughly dry, glue a small piece of touch-and-close fastening (velcro) to the front board and the back of the clasp to act as a fastening. The book is now ready to use.

address book with notepad

make a large address book to keep beside the telephone,
or a small portable version like the one pictured.
Either way, you will find it effective and easy to use,
having designed it to your own specifications.

The example here is covered with alphabet paper made from a photocopied collage overlaid with handmade Japanese paper. This can be personalized with your or a friend's initials, drawings, maps, or a simple repeat pattern. If you cover the book with paper and are going to use it every day, a slipcase (as described in the chapter on containers) would slow wear and tear to prolong its life; or you could use a bookcloth for extra strength and durability. There is the additional advantage of having a removable notebook with tear-off pages for quick notes and telephone messages, and when the pages run out, simply add more; you could also use the pocket for maps, guides, stamps, or business cards. The tabs are unmarked in the model, but you can organize and label your index by collage, calligraphy, or typed symbols to suit your needs.

The size of the example here is 5⁵⁄₁₆ x 4½ x ¾ inches.

1 Fold and cut paper for pages and make eight sections with three folds in each. Align and trim the fore edges. Then cut one fold for each section, using heavy paper, the same height and ⅝ inch wider than the page size (A).

A

2 Cut the folds as shown to form the index and place in the center of each section.

3 Sew the book onto tapes (three in this example) as described in Sewing on Tapes, page 48.

4 Make the notepad by cutting single sheets of paper roughly the same size as the book and gluing them together at one end.

5 Cut a piece of the heavy paper the same size as the notepad. Lay a sheet of waste paper ⅜ inch away from the glued edge of the pad, brush the exposed edge with glue and attach the heavy paper. Press.

MATERIALS

Paper for pages

Heavy paper for index, pocket, and note pad

Decorative cover paper

Opaque Japanese paper for cover

Endpapers

Sewing thread

Mull and kraft paper

Waxed paper

Sewing tapes

Craft glue

Wheatflour paste

EQUIPMENT

Knife and/or scalpel

Cutting mat and board

Dividers

Steel safety ruler

Bone folder

Pressing boards

Paste brushes

Sewing needle

6

Cut a piece of the Japanese cover paper the same height as the notepad (A), adding on the spine thickness (B) and ¾ inch (C), then glue it to the heavy paper backing. Trim the notepad ¼ inch smaller than the book on the three unglued edges.

8

Score the lines with a bone folder, crease to form the pocket folds and turn-ins as shown, then glue (D) to (E) and press.

7

Make the pocket from cloth, heavy paper, or lined plain paper, and cut to size as shown in the diagram.

(A)	=	Half the height of the notepad
(B)	=	The width of the notepad plus ⅜ inch.
(C)	=	The thickness of the notepad plus ⅛ inch
(D)	=	⅜-inch turn-in
(E)	=	(A) (Proportions not exact on diagram)
(F)	=	1-inch turn-in

9

Cut one endpaper for the back of the book as usual. The front endpaper needs an extra width of paper to accommodate the thickness of the notepad (B). Measure and cut accordingly. Attach the endpapers with glue.

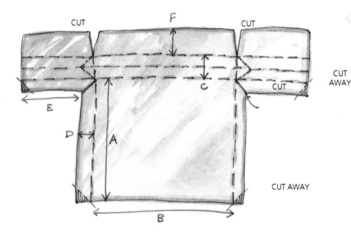

10

Trim the inner fold of each endpaper back to the width of the book to expose the index tabs (A).

11

Apply glue to the spine of the book, trim the head and tail if required, and line the spine with mull and kraft paper as described in the Case Binding project on page 62. Trim the mull and tapes to an equal width using a piece of board to protect your endpapers.

11

Make a collage using paper large enough to cover the book with approximately ¾ inch extra for turn-ins. Photocopy it (or use another decorative paper that won't smudge when damp), apply wheatflour paste to it, and lay the Japanese paper over it, rubbing down well. Place blotting paper on each side and press. Then leave to dry between pressing boards and under a weight, changing the blotting paper frequently until it is dry.

13

Cut two cover boards ¼ inch longer than the height of the book and ⅛ inch narrower than the width. Place the notepad and pocket on top of the book with a cover board on each side. Measure the combined thickness (A) for the width of the spine piece, which will be the same height as the cover boards. Make the case as described on page 64.

14

Paste and put down the back endpaper as usual, press, and leave it weighted to dry. Lay the book on the back board and drop the front board back. Paste the endpaper then stand the book on its spine. Put the endpaper down with the board open as shown, supporting the book block with a weight. Make sure the endpaper is worked into the joint (A) and forms a right angle with the book without pulling. Cover with waxed or blotting paper, a pressing board, and weight, and leave to dry in the open position.

15

When the endpaper is completely dry, glue in the pocket. Once the glue dries, place the notepad in the pocket. The book is now ready to use.

poem book

the poem book is designed to reveal each page in sequence,but it **can also be read, fully extended, in a different order.** The text in the poem book below comes from nineteenth- century book catalogues that were cut up to create a new story, and is sandwiched between two sheets of thin acetate that are machine sewn together.

Alternatively, you could attach the panels using wire, rivets, or eyelets, and thread various materials or wires through the holes. You can use collage, calligraphy, photocopies, or a typewriter to produce your text (and/or images), which can be constructed like the example here or glued to panels of decorative or handmade paper. Although the structure is called a poem book, it would work equally well with photographs, prints, or drawings as a hanging book or frame. You can experiment with the shape of the windows; the format stays the same.

The size of this poem book is 3¾ x 3 x 1⅛ inches when closed, and 11¾ x 12 x ¹⁄₁₆ inches when fully open.

1

Choose your poem or text. Arrange the text in panels and mount each one on decorative paper with glue or sew them between two layers of acetate. In the example, the threads are left uncut as part of the design, but they can be knotted and trimmed as you prefer.

2

Cut a piece of paper and mark with the same number of panels as your text. Set the text panels over the paper in the pattern you desire, vertically, horizontally, in a particular order, or none at all. Use the paper to experiment with cuts and folds until you have the pattern you want. This example uses two T-shaped cuts as shown, to help fold the book up neatly.

3

Cut the greyboard into the required number of pieces for the panels, allowing for a frame of at least ⅜ to ⅝ inch around each piece of text (A). The boards should all be the same size. Measure the largest piece of text and leave a small margin around it (B), then cut windows from each board to this measurement (C).

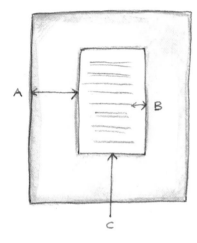

4

Cut small strips of the covering paper and cover the inner corners of the windows as described in step 10 of the Journal project on page 102.

step 10 of the Journal project on page 102.

MATERIALS

Text and/or images

Thin acetate, or decorative/handmade paper

Thin greyboard

Cover paper

Lining paper

Colored threads (for machine and hand sewing)

Waxed paper for pressing

Craft glue

EQUIPMENT

Knife and/or scalpel

Cutting mat or board

Bone folder

Dividers

Sewing needle

Sewing machine (optional)

Glue brush

Pressing boards

The example on page 130 is made from six pairs of jointed boards attached to each other by paper hinges. To make each pair, cut a piece of the cover paper big enough to cover two boards with a ⅛-inch gap between (A) and allowing for a ⅝-inch turn-in around the outside edge (B).

Glue down the boards, leaving a ⅛-inch joint allowance, or more for thick paper. If you are unsure about the right allowance to leave, fold a piece of the cover paper around two board thicknesses and crease. Add to this three thicknesses of lining paper and a little extra for the sewing (or more if you are using wire or rivets to attach the text panels).

Glue down the turn-ins at the board edges and the windows as described in step 12 for the "Journal," on page 102.

Make hinges from cloth or paper by folding the material in half and gluing it together. Then cut the hinges ⅛ inch narrower than the panel at the head and tail (A). Glue one side of the hinge to one of the pairs.

Join the hinge to another pair of boards, allowing extra space between to accommodate a lining paper. Make sure there is no strain. The width of the hinges will vary, depending on the number of boards they have to fold around and what method you use to attach the text panels. In the poem book on page 130, for example, three of the hinges wrap around two board thicknesses (A), and two of them have to accommodate three boards

8

The fully extended model looks like this, with the hinges identified as described in the previous instruction.

9

After the panels are joined together, line them with your chosen paper, following step 12 of the Journal project, but this time taking the lining paper across any joints. Take extra care in rubbing down the paper between the joints or the book won't shut properly. Leave under a weight between waxed paper and pressing boards to dry.

10

Attach your poem or text to the back of each panel using decorative stitches, knots, thin wire, or rivets.

11

Fold up your book and tie with cord or ribbon if you are including this in the design.

12

If you prefer, the text (or photographs, drawings, etc.) can be sandwiched between two sets of windows, but you will have to allow twice as much material for each hinge and at the board joints. If you decide to use this method, make two sets of windows following steps 4 to 7, and glue the panels with the text or image between. Press and leave to dry between waxed paper under weighted boards.

rebinding a book

there is no need to replace a favorite book
because it is falling apart.
You can repair it and turn it into a unique binding using
many of the techniques illustrated in this book.

The model shown here is a binding of *Alice in Wonderland* and *Alice through the Looking-Glass* sewn on wrapped raised cords. It has a window in the back board and onlays of Mexican bark paper. If you want to repair an old book that has lost its binding and don't want to include any artwork, follow steps 1 through 4 of this project, and then follow steps 1 through 16 of the Case Binding project on page 62. Finally, you can make a slipcase to protect your book as described on page 88 or perhaps a Japanese-style wraparound case as shown on pages 38–40.

The size of the book here is 8¹⁄₁₆ x 5½ x 1⅜ inches.

1 Take the book apart by first cutting the sewing threads in the middle of each signature carefully.

2 Place the book between pressing boards with a weight on top, leaving the spine protruding a little. For older books glued with animal glues, apply a thick layer of wheatflour paste to soften the old glue and leave to soak for a few minutes. Remove the old glue with a bone folder, being careful not to damage the damp paper. Remove all old sewing threads, tapes, and lining materials as well. This method is not suitable for modern books with hot-melt adhesives on the spine.

3 Cut tissue guards to repair the sections, one for each signature (in the example on page 134 they are made from a thin Indian handmade paper) slightly longer than the height and approximately ¾ inch wider than the thickness of each signature. If you are repairing a book, you don't want the guards to show, so use a subtle Japanese tissue to match the book paper.

4 Lay the guards on a smooth work surface and apply paste to them one at a time. Attach to each signature, rub down well and leave to dry. You may find it easier to lay the guard on clean waxed paper once it is pasted and use the paper to wrap the guard around the signature to keep your hands clean. When the guards are dry, wrap the signatures in waxed paper and press overnight.

5

Make holes in the signatures for sewing on cords, as described in steps 1 through 3 of Sewing over Cords or Thongs, page 50. The thread used in the model has been waxed and is wrapped around the cords a few times between coming out and going back into the sewing hole because the signatures are thick and a solid, red line was desired as part of the design.

6

Then cut two endpapers slightly larger than the size of the book and tip them on as described in Attaching Endpapers, page 58. For extra strength, the blank leaf at the beginning of the book can be pasted to the first blank sheet of the book if there is one and pressed, using blotting paper to absorb some of the moisture. Change the blotting paper at regular intervals until the endpapers are dry. Trim to size.

7

Plan your design and cutouts since they need to be made before the boards are attached and covered. The circle used in the book on page 134 is a representation of either the rabbit hole or the looking-glass and has Alice, the Mad Hatter, and the Cheshire Cat sandwiched between two sheets of acetate so you can see through to the other side. You can interpret your chosen book in many ways. For example, you could use the title as the design by enlarging and juggling the letter forms, or play around with embossing, illustrate a character, or layer and sculpt the boards by using onlays. There is no right or wrong aspect for your design; just choose one you are interested in.

8

Cut four thin pieces of greyboard ⅛ inch larger than the book at the head, tail, and fore edge.

Once you have finalized your design, you can construct your cover boards. First, make the windows through the boards. Then glue on any raised elements of the design to the outer boards (see the Diary with a Clasp project on page 122 for instructions on embossing) and make any necessary artwork, collage, or onlays.

Lay one of the inner boards in position with the covered edge in line with the back of the book. Fan out the cords and glue them to the boards. Repeat with the other board, then press with waxed paper and leave to dry under weighted boards.

Cut two pieces of the colored guard paper ¾ inch longer than the height of the board, and ⅝ inch wide. Glue to the spine edge of the inner boards (A) and fold around board edges at head and tail (B). Snip into the corners on both sides of the board and glue down the turn-ins (C).

A

C

B

If you have cut windows into the boards, transfer their size and position to the endpaper by using a sharp pencil.

Cover the edges of any windows on the inner and outer boards with a strip of the colored guard paper; snip and glue down to the board surfaces.

Cover the outer boards with your chosen material, pressing with a piece of sponge if you are embossing (see Diary with a Clasp, page 122). Trim the turn-ins to ¾ inch on all four edges and cut the corners at the spine edge as indicated (A). Glue this turn-in down, but leave the other three sides unglued at this point. The boards in the example on page 134 have their edges covered in paper to match the guards, with a panel of bark paper over the top. If you are using acetate between the cutouts, turn in the cover paper before gluing the boards together. If you just want a hole through the board to reveal an image on the endpaper, turn in the cover paper after the boards are laminated.

15

Lay your collage of images between the acetate sheets (cut slightly larger than the window) and position it on the inner board. Glue the outer boards and position them exactly over the top of the inner board. Press and leave the book to dry under a weight between waxed paper and pressing boards.

16

Trim the corners as usual and glue down the turn-ins over the laminated board edges.

17

Prepare any other artwork you need for the cover. The book on page 134 has two onlays made from bark paper. Eyelets are applied with an eyelet punch and the "eat me" and "drink me" labels are threaded through and glued to the inside of the board.

18

Put a piece of waste board between the endpapers and support the cover board using pressing boards. Then cut out any windows previously marked. Also trim a sliver of paper away from the fore edge of the endpapers to allow for any stretch when pasted. Put down the endpapers as described in "Case Binding" on page 62. Press and leave to dry under a weight between waxed paper and pressing boards.

suppliers

Aiko's Art Materials Import, Inc.
3347 North Clark Street
Chicago, IL 60657
ph: (773) 404-5600
*Aiko's carries bookbinding
supplies and materials, all sorts
of Japanese handmade papers,
and other art supplies.*

Binders Discount Art Center
P.O. Box 53097
Atlanta, GA 30355
ph: (800) 877-3242
fax: (800) 872-0294
*This catalogue carries a nice
selection of fine art papers,
including various Thai Chiri, Thai
reversible, and French marbled
papers in many beautiful
patterns and colors. Also
available are art boards and all
other basic art supplies, such as
brushes, tools, adhesives, and
paints.*

Daniel Smith
4150 First Avenue South
P.O. Box 84268
Seattle, WA 98124-5568
ph: (800) 426-6740
fax: (800) 238-4065
*This Seattle store and mail order
catalogue carries various
boards, papers, knives,
adhesives (including
wheatpaste), and most other art
supplies. Call for a catalogue.*

Dick Blick Art Materials
P.O. Box 1267
Galesburg, IL 61402-1267
ph: (800) 447-8192
*This mail order catalogue stocks
a wide variety of papers and
boards, including kraft and
utility papers; tape and glue;
X-Acto knives and cutting
boards; various threads, cords,
strings, and laces; brushes and
tools; paints; and most other
art supplies. Call for their
extensive catalogue.*

Nancy's Notions
333 Biechl Avenue
P.O. Box 683
Beaver Dam, WI 53916-0683
ph: (800) 833-0690
fax: (800) 255-8119
*Nancy's Notions sells a wide
variety of sewing supplies,
many of which are useful for
the bookbinder: threads,
including metallic and other
decorative threads; fabrics;
papers, including non-acid
tissue paper; and decorative
ribbons, and buttons. Call for a
catalogue.*

New York Central Art Supply
62 Third Avenue
New York, NY 10003
toll-free ph: (800) 950-6111
within NY state: (212) 477-0400
fax: (212) 475-2513
*The New York Central store
stocks most art supplies and the
company also has a mail order
catalogue you can request. In
addition, they have a large fine
art paper department that has
its own extensive catalogue,
carrying decorative and archival
quality papers plus papers from
Thailand, Japan, India, Egypt,
Europe, Nepal, and the
Philippines.*

Pearl Paint Art and Craft Center
308 Canal Street
New York, NY 10013
ph: (800) 221-6845
*Pearl has stores in locations all
over the country, including
California, Florida, Georgia,
Illinois, Maryland,
Massachusetts, New Jersey,
Pennsylvania, Texas, and
Virginia. The staff is
knowledgeable, and the
company stocks most every art
supply you can think of,
including papers, boards,
paints, brushes, tools, and craft
items. Call for a mail order
catalogue and list of other store
locations.*

Swallow Creek Papers
P.O. Box 152
Spring Mills, PA 16875
ph: (814) 422-8651
*Decorative papers for all
papercrafts, including hand-
marbled and paste papers. Also
sells paper marbling supplies.*

Papersource Inc
730 N Franklin, Suite 111
Chicago, IL 60610

Sam Flax
111, 8th Avenue
New York, NY10011

Paper Art Company
7240 Shadeland Station
Suite 300
Indianapolis, IN 46256

Decorative Papers
PO Box 749
Easthampton, MA10027

U.S.
Alvin & Co. Inc.
Box 188, Windsor, CT
06095; 2418 Teagarden St,
San Leandro, CA 94577

Arthur Brown & Bro. Inc.
2 W. 46th Street
New York, NY 10036

Connoisseur Studios
Box 7187
Louisville, KY 40207

Dahle (USA)
6 Benson Road
Oxford, CT 06483

Duro Art Supply Co. Inc.
1832 Juneway Terrace
Chicago, IL 60626

Faber Castell Corp.
41 Dickerson Street
Newark, NJ 07107

Gramercy Corp.
1145 A. W. Custer Place
Denver, CO 80223

M. Grumbacher Inc.
460 West 34th Street
New York, NY 10001

Loew-Correll Inc.
131 W. Rugby Avenue
Palisades Park, NJ 07650

The Morilla Co. Inc.
43-01 21st Street
Long Island City, NY 11101

Permanent Pigments Inc.
2700 Highland Avenue
Cincinnati, OH 45212

F. Weber Co.
Wayne & Windrim Avenues
Philadelphia, PA 19144

Winsor & Newton Inc.
555 Winsor Drive
Secaucus, NJ 07094

Yasutomo & Co.
24 California Street
San Francisco, CA 94111

CANADA
Artist Gallery
3350 Fairview Street
Burlington, Ont. L7N 3L5

Mona Lisa Art Salon Ltd.
1518 7th Street
SW Calgary, Alberta T2R 1A7

Pro-Graphics Ltd.
6019 4th Street
SE Calgary, Alberta T2H 2A5

The Art Store
10054 108th Street
Edmonton, Alberta T5J 3S7

Rapid Blueprint Inc.
P.O. Box 306
35 King William Street
Hamilton, Ont. L8N 3G5

Hunt Canada International
5940 Ambler Drive
Mississauga, Ont.
L4W 2N3

Maritime Graphic Arts Ltd.
1730 Granville Street
Halifax, Nova Scotia
B3J 1X5

Wallack's Ltd.
231 Bank Street
Ottawa, Ont.

Norcal Reprographics Ltd.
1180 Winnipeg Street
Regina, Saskatchewan
S4R 1J6

M. Francis Kelly Ltd.
P.O. Box 5715
5c Golf Avenue
St. Johns, Newfoundland
A1C 5W8

Curry's Art Store Ltd.
756 Yonge Street
Toronto, Ont. M4Y 2B9

Loomis & Toles Company
963 Eglinton Avenue E
Toronto, Ont. M4G 4B5

Lynrich Arts Enterprises Ltd.
64 Gerrard Street E
Toronto, Ont. M5B 1G5

Selectone Paint Ltd.
39 Gail Grove
Toronto, Ont. M9M 1M5

Hansen's Art Supplies
1130 Robson Street
Vancouver, B.C. V6E 1B2

Maxwell Artists Materials Ltd.
601 West Cordova Street
Vancouver, B.C. V6B 1G1

Island Blueprint Co. Ltd.
905F, Fort Street
Victoria, V8V 3K3

Fraser Art Supplies Ltd.
414 Graham Avenue
Winnipeg, Manitoba
R3C 0L8

Lewis Art Supplies
1438 Erin Street
Winnipeg, Manitoba
R3E 2S8

selected bibliography

Chambers, Anne.
A Practical Guide to Marbling Paper.
Thames & Hudson,
London. 1986

Chambers, Anne.
Suminagashi.
The Japanese Art of Marbling.
Thames and Hudson, London.
1991

Cockerell, D.
Bookbinding and the Care of Books.
Pitman, London and New York.
1963

Ikegami, Kojiro.
Japanese Bookbinding.
Weatherhill, New York. 1986

Ipert, Stephane & Rousseau, Florent.
Simple Decorative Paper Techniques. Search Press, London.1992

Johnson, Arthur W.
Thames and Hudson Manual of Bookbinding.
Thames and Hudson, London.1978

La Plantz, Shereen.
Cover to Cover.
Lark Books, 1995

Larbalestier, Simon.
The Art and Craft of Montage.
Mitchell Beazley,
London. 1993

Middleton, Bernard.
A History of English Craft Bookbinding Technique.
Hafner Press, London. 1963

Ploughman, John
The Craft of Handmade Paper.
Apple Press, London. 1997

Robinson, Ivor
Introducing Bookbinding.
Oxford Polytechnic Press,
London and New York. 1984

Saddington, Marianne.
Making your own paper.
New Holland Ltd, London. 1990

Shannon, Faith.
The Art and Craft of Paper.
Mitchell Beazley,
London. 1987

Smith, Keith A.
Non-Adhesive Binding Volume 1.
Books Without Paste or Glue.
Keith Smith Books, New York.
1993

Smith, Keith A.
Non-Adhesive Binding Volume 2.
1,2 & 3 Section Sewings.
Keith Smith Books, New York.
1995

Smith, Keith A.
Non-Adhesive Binding Volume 3. Exposed Spine Sewings.
Keith Smith Books, New York.
1996

Smith, Keith A.
Structure of the Visual Book.
Keith Smith Books, New York.
1994

Smith, Keith A.
Text in the Book Format.
Keith Smith Books, New York.
1995

Smith, Philip.
The Book:Art and Object.
Philip Smith, Merstham. 1992

Smith, Philip.
New Directions in Bookbinding.
Studio Vista,
London and New York. 1974

The New Bookbinder.
The Journal of Designer Bookbinders Volumes 1-17.
Published annually by
Designer Bookbinders, London.

Turner, Silvie.
Which Paper?
Estamp, London. 1991

Turner, Silvie and Birgit Skiold.
Handmade Paper Today.
Lund Humphries, London. 1985
Watson, David.

Creative Handmade Paper.
Search Press, London. 1991

Williams, Nancy.
Paperwork.
Phaidon Press, London. 1993

Credits

Gallery 1 (pages 34-35)
Left to Right: Mary Deakin "Tyger, Tyger" by William Blake; Sue Doggett "Eel Corridor"
"The Cheese Musem," Flutter Book; Fold-Out Book

Gallery 2 (pages 44-45)
Left to Right: Clare Bryan "Forbidden Fruit," (Top to Bottom) Emma Ruffle, Sue Doggett, Emma Ruffle, Emma Ruffle, Sue Doggett; Sue Doggett "Serpents and Skulls," Emma Ruffle; Sue Doggett

Gallery 3 (pages 70-71)
Left to Right: Vivien Frank "Bestiary," Sue Doggett; (standing) Sue Doggett, (flat) Penny Stanford; (Top to bottom) Vivien Frank, Vivien Frank, Sue Doggett; Sue Doggett

Gallery 4 (pages 80-81)
Left to Right: (left) Sue Whittington (Right) Margaret Benson; Clare Bryan "Alice in Wonderland," Sue Doggett; Sue Doggett "Inamorato," (left) Helen Hutchins, (right) Penny Stanford

Gallery 5 (pages 92-93)
Left to Right: Clare Bryan "Open Closed," Clare Bryan "Open Closed," Helen Hutchins; Emma Ruffle; Sue Doggett "Mr Palomar's Library"

acknowledgments

I would like to thank the following people for their support over the years and during the writing of this book.

To all my teachers and colleagues for introducing me to the book as an exciting medium with which to work, also for sharing their hard earned knowledge and creative energy with me and hundreds of other students.
Thanks go especially to Ivor Robinson, who has taught me so much, helped me out of sticky situations, and gave me my first teaching job. To members of Designer Bookbinders who have offered advice and support, particularly David Sellars, Jenni Grey, and Faith Shannon (who taught me how to make the majority of bindings in this book), Jen Lindsay, Romilly Saumarez-Smith, and Philip Smith, all of whom have been hugely influential creatively as colleagues and as friends.

Special thanks to Maggie Chandler who was so supportive as a colleague and so generous in sharing her teaching methods with me. Thanks also to her, for showing me how to make the "Wraparound Book" (page 38) and the "Limp Paper Binding" (page 66).

Many thanks to Hedi Kyle whose "Flag Book" (page 76) and "Everlasting Fold Book" (page 28) are included with her kind permission. Thanks to people like Hedi Kyle for popularizing book structures like the "Star Book" and the "Theater Book," which are now standards in the book artist's repertoire.

Thanks to all the past and present students who kindly lent work to be photographed for this book, and special thanks to Pauline Brown for suggesting the thread work on the "Foldout Book" (page 31), which I have also incorporated in the "Poem Book."

Kind thanks to Rob Shepherd of Shepherd Bookbinders Ltd., for lending materials and equipment for the photographs in the introductory chapters.

Many thanks to Emma Ruffle of John Purcell Paper for advice and suggestions on interesting and unusual papers.

Thanks to my family for supporting and encouraging me always, and to Clare for her artistic support and advice.

Finally, a grateful and very special thanks to Jonathan for his constant support, enthusiasm, and patience, and for keeping my confidence going.

index